Also by Kathryn Petras and Ross Petras

Unusually
Stupid
Americans

Unusually
Stupid
Americans

A Compendium of
All-American Stupidity

Kathryn Petras and
Ross Petras

Villard / New York

LIBRARY OF CONGRESS CATALOGING-IN-PUBLICATION DATA
Unusually stupid Americans: a compendium of all-American
    stupidity / [compiled by] Kathryn Petras and Ross Petras.
    p. cm.
    ISBN 0-8129-7082-9 (trade paperback)
    1. Stupidity—United States—Anecdotes. I. Petras, Kathryn.
    II. Petras, Ross.
    BF431.U65 2003
    081—dc21   2003053753

Villard Books website address: www.villard.com

Printed in the United States of America

987654

Acknowledgments

Many thanks to Ann Godoff, for conceiving the idea; to Bruce Tracy, for being a wonderful editor, as always—and for the delicious skordalia; and to all the keen-eyed people who've written and e-mailed us over the years with their thousands of examples of stupidity!

Contents

Introduction

The United States of America has long been considered a beacon of democracy, a melting pot—where people of all ethnicities, races, colors, and creeds live together, work together, and play together.

This is, of course, a good thing. We take no exception to said melting-pot analogy. We may all agree that the U.S.A. is indeed a melting pot, a splendid stew of different people.

But the astute individual may realize that in this melting pot there are *lumps*, as it were . . . or perhaps clumps. Clods, chunks, whatever one cares to term it, of stupidity. Unusually *American* stupidity.

Red, white, and blue stupidity emanates from our government, our institutions, our businesses, our celebrities, and even from just plain regular people. And this, as you might expect, is what *Unusually Stupid Americans* examines. As proud Americans, we feel it incumbent upon us to celebrate this oft-overlooked area of Americana.

What constitutes an Unusually Stupid American? Any number of criteria apply—for just as there are many different types of Americans, there are many different types of stupidity.

In some cases, the stupidity derives from an innate combination of genetics and fate—i.e., stupid brain meets stupid situation, and stupidity ensues. We term this "the idiot next door" behavior. In other cases, overweening greed or ambition overrides common sense. (This is the case with many of our politicians, public officials, and corporate leaders.) Sometimes stupidity arises out of our wonderful democratic institutions—when in their estimable efforts to be "fair" or "open-minded" they succeed instead in being stupid. (This explains the rash of political correctness, et al.) Other times, stupidity arises from the marvelous American optimism that refuses to acknowledge that a particular product/service/idea/etc. had never been thought of before for one very good reason (viz., it was stupid).

Ultimately, of course, American stupidity is as unique as the U.S.A. itself—a rich and uncategorizable hodgepodge, a stew . . . a melting pot. As Justice Potter Stewart once said about obscenity, "I know it when I see it." The same applies to hard-core American stupidity (about which, to the best of our knowledge, the learned judge made no comment).

So let others talk about the shining moments in politics, business, and life in these United States. To paraphrase William Shakespeare (who was not an American) in his play about Julius Caesar (who was also not American), we come not to praise the U.S.A. but to talk about its lumps, its chunks, its clumps, and, yes, its clods.

Unusually
Stupid
Americans

Stupid Education in the U.S.A.

"**T**hose who can, do; those who can't, teach." Thus goes the old saying. We take exception to this, as there are many fine teachers and other educators out there who are certainly doing a great deal—and a great deal of good.

Of course, there's a flip side to this. . . .

Bad Moments in Innovative Education

We Americans are innovators; we don't like doing stuff the old ways; we proudly invent new ways of doing everything. And today's modern American teachers are innovators like everyone else—they boldly try to get kids interested in school by throwing away the textbooks and introducing new, fun, exciting, *different* ways of learning. But maybe, just maybe, there's something to be said for just reading the dull old textbooks, as these innovative teaching disasters show.

Teacher innovatively uses banana prop in sex ed

Students learned one thing from this class: Mood music,

bananas, and sex ed don't mix. A teacher at Gulf Coast High School in Naples, Florida, decided to put on a demonstration of safe-sex practices. A laudable idea. He picked two volunteers, a boy and a girl, to come up in front of the class. Then he dimmed the lights and put on some "mood music": Christmas carols. (It was the only music he had.) He gave the boy the banana and told him to hold it while the girl gently put a condom over it. Some of the kids in class weren't amused; nor were parents when they found out about it; and nor, for that matter, were school administrators. As the teacher put it, "It wasn't merely a demonstration of how to place a condom over a banana." No, indeed. School officials decided to flunk the sex-ed teacher: They fired him.

Teacher innovatively feeds cute puppies to giant snakes in bio class

In retrospect, it was not one of the better ideas in biology pedagogy. A teacher at the Bluestem High School in Kansas who kept two boa constrictors wanted to show students how snakes eat. Three puppies were donated by a school-board member who operates a shelter where dogs are put to sleep. The problem was that the puppies were "soft" and "cuddly," and people got very upset about the planned demonstration—the idea of cute puppies yelping in pain while being squeezed to death didn't sit well with them. They began complaining loudly, and there were suggestions that the teacher be fired. The teacher defended his actions but realized he might have been a bit . . . insensitive. "I'm not sure I considered the sensitivity of some people when it involved what's considered a pet." But he also defended his choice of doomed puppies, saying, "I hate to see any life wasted." But now he's trying to find nonsnake-owning homes for the puppies.

Math worksheets innovatively ask the question: "How many bazookas does it take . . . ?"

The idea that learning must be fun has taken over the education industry, but there are limits—which were reached with math worksheets published by a Minnesota company called MindWare. In 2001, education officials complained that math worksheets for 12-year-olds contained jokes about unruly kids being shot. Another, called Five Foolish Rabbits, had a farmer using different kinds of weapons like bazookas to wipe out rabbits eating his crops. The company president said the worksheets were supposed to "liven up" math.

Teacher innovatively adds roadkill to curriculum

The fact that North Shore Technical High School of Middleton, Massachusetts, didn't have a taxidermy course didn't stop a bold, innovative carpentry teacher and amateur taxidermist from deciding to give the kids a little lesson in skinning animals for fun and profit. Finding a dead coyote on the side of the road on March 15, 2003, the intrepid teacher tossed it into his pickup and brought it to school—and skinned it outside, to show his pupils just how it was done. The aftermath of this school exercise was more painful: Although the brain of the coyote was too deteriorated to tell if it had rabies, two students opted for vaccinations, just in case. Superintendent Amy O'Malley said the entire incident was under investigation and added, "Of course, this was not a school-sanctioned activity."

Science exhibit innovatively teaches "grossology"

It's supposed to be the latest thing in "science" education: highlighting the gross aspects. In 2001, at a Chicago exhibition about the human body, children were treated to a vomit machine and a fart pinball game and a huge, sneezing nose. The exhibit organizers said, "There's a lot of yelling and screaming." And, supposedly, a lot of learning, although what kind of learning is perhaps more problematic. According to the organizer, " 'We smell the butt!' becomes a 4th-grader's Eureka! moment."

College teacher innovatively teaches with rotting animals

Artist Ben Jennings wanted to capture the essence of decay for students in his art class at the University of Wisconsin–Marathon County. What better way than to put up an art display featuring a disemboweled raccoon and a dead crow? Unfortunately for the intrepid art teacher, school officials objected to the smell. Said Dean Jim Veninga, "I sort of like raccoons, but I don't want them in the university's gallery, dead or alive." Jennings defended the project, insisting that "it wasn't to be disgusting or grotesque." Nevertheless, it ended up behind the college greenhouse—on a compost heap.

Roll the "probability cubes" and hope for a lucky seven! Probability cubes? That's what math teachers in the U.S. are now encouraged to call dice, which are used in class to teach various probability concepts. Apparently, calling dice "dice" encourages gambling.

"Is Our Children Learning?"

As we know, President George W. Bush asked this rhetorical question during his first campaign for the presidency.
Unfortunately, perhaps they is not. . . .

- Number of correct answers out of 100 needed to get an A on the Palm Beach County final exam in history (for high school seniors): 50

  Number of answers to get a B: 39

  Number of correct answers to pass: 23

- Percentage of U.S. citizens ages 18–24 in 2002 (post-9/11) who couldn't find Afghanistan on a map: 83%

  Percentage who couldn't identify Israel: 85%

  Percentage who could correctly place the 2001 *Survivor* TV series island in the South Pacific: 86%

  Percentage who couldn't find the U.K.: 69%

  Percentage who couldn't find France: 65%

  Percentage who couldn't find Japan: 58%

  Percentage who couldn't find the Pacific Ocean: 29%

  Percentage who couldn't find the U.S.: 11%

  Rank of U.S. respondents compared with those of the other 8 countries polled: second to last

  Rank of U.S. respondents in estimating the population of the U.S.: last

  —National Geographic 2002 Global Geographic Literacy Survey

- Percentage of high school seniors who thought that Italy, Germany, or Japan was a U.S. ally in World War II: over 50%

  Percentage of high school seniors who thought the Gulf of Tonkin agreement ended the Korean War: 43%

  —2001 U.S. History National Assessment of Education Progress Survey

- Percentage of 17-year-olds who correctly placed the Civil War in the period 1850–1900: 33%

  Percentage who thought the Civil War happened in the 18th century: more than 25%

  Percentage who correctly identified Abraham Lincoln as the author of the Emancipation Proclamation: 66%

  Percentage who said Lincoln wrote the Bill of Rights: 14%

  Percentage who said Lincoln wrote the Missouri Compromise: 10%

  Percentage who said Lincoln wrote the abolitionist novel *Uncle Tom's Cabin*: 9%

  —*Wilson Quarterly* 24, no. 2 (spring 2000), quoting a national assessment test given in the late 1980s

- Percentage of college seniors at the 55 top colleges in the country who knew that the phrase "Government of the people, by the people, for the people" comes from Lincoln's Gettysburg Address: 22%

  Percentage who could identify James Madison as the "Father of the Constitution": 23%

Percentage who could identify and correctly place in time the Reconstruction: 29%

Percentage who knew George Washington was the American general at the Battle of Yorktown: 33%

Percentage who were familiar with the name "Snoop Doggy Dogg" and could identify him as a rapper: 98%

Percentage who knew Beavis and Butt-head are cartoon characters: 99%

—2000 American Council of Trustees and Alumni (ACTA) survey (asking questions culled from high school textbooks)

• Percentage of Ivy League students who didn't know the name of the U.S. Speaker of the House: 44%

Percentage who couldn't identify the chairman of the Federal Reserve Board: 35%

Percentage who didn't know how many U.S. Supreme Court justices there are: 23%

—*Reader's Digest*, September 1993

The Two Stupidest Education Lawsuits

1. If You Don't Get an A+, Sue the School

This is what Memphis High School student Brian Delekta is doing, filing suit against the entire school district and the principal. As part of the school's "outside experience" module, Brian had worked in his mother's law office as a paralegal. She gave him an A+. Unfortunately, the highest grade

the school accepts is an A, which is what Brian got on his report card, regardless of Mom's A+. So Brian and his mom
did the natural thing: They decided to sue for the A+, plus
$25,000 in damages.

2. If the Course Is Too Hard, Sue the School

Southern Methodist University's Advanced Education Center in Houston offered a Microsoft computer-certification
course. Twelve students who took—and failed—this course
sued the university, claiming that administrators had promised them it would be easy.

Facts from Stupid Textbooks; or, What You Learned in High School Was Very Probably Wrong

A recent high school textbook devoted only six lines to the
illustrious father of our country (George Washington, in
case you're wondering) but six and a half *pages* to Marilyn
Monroe, who of course needs no introduction. Another recent textbook has a math problem that begins with a
sneaker commercial: "Will is saving his allowance to buy a
pair of Nike™ shoes that cost $68.25. If Will is making
$3.25 a week. . . ."

With low standards like this, it's no wonder many modern textbooks are also filled with typos, misleading state-
ments, and just plain errors. Do the authors care? At least
one doesn't. One of the authors of Houghton Mifflin's *History of the United States* said he didn't know that there were
accuracy problems in his book. No wonder—he didn't even
try to see a final manuscript. "For me to read the book and

A BURNING QUESTION . . .

Is the ability to read a necessity to be able to graduate from high school? Perhaps not if you're a student in Des Moines, Iowa, and if 40-year teaching vet and candidate for the city's school board James Patch has his way. He feels that students shouldn't have to be able to read to get a diploma, as this is discriminatory against those with dyslexia. In his words, "I would like to see us be accountable, but as far as tying graduation to reading, we're going to have a lot of architects and artists and doctors out there who aren't going to graduate from high school if we do that."

check it for factual accuracy simply makes no sense," the concerned teacher said.

No sense? Here's a collection of "facts" as found in various textbooks that are or were in print in the 1990s or early 2000s. They've been culled from various angry articles, reviews, or e-mails; in some cases, the "facts" have been somewhat condensed, but it was all what was reported in the press—it's all true, and that's a fact, not a "fact."

"Fact" 1

Columbus set sail in 1942.

The True Fact: Try a few hundred years earlier, in 1492. (This egregious typo was reported in *Reader's Digest.*)

"Fact" 2

Sputnik was the Soviet Union's first intercontinental ballistic missile armed with a nuclear warhead.

The True Fact: Try satellite, not missile; try no warhead, just a thing that made a beeping sound. This "fact" was found in *American Odyssey,* published by Glencoe.

"Fact" 3

"Frankenstein pieced together the parts of dead bodies. Finally he brought a creature to life. But Frankenstein's creation was an eight foot monster. Eventually the monster destroyed the biologist."

The True Fact: This interesting tidbit of biology history appeared in the Fearon *Biology* textbook as if it were a fact, a discussion about a real biologist. Maybe it was meant to be motivational: If you study hard enough, you, too, can be a mad scientist. Students were not told that Dr. Frankenstein was not a real biologist and that he actually didn't create an eight-foot monster in Transylvania after all.

"Fact" 4

Australia is part of South and Southeast Asia.

The True Fact: Australia is actually a separate continent. It belongs to the region called, interestingly enough, "Australia." (This appeared in Fearon's *Global Studies* textbook.)

"Fact" 5

"You can't walk or even push your way through most of the rain forest."

The True Fact: Actually, most portions of the rain forest are very easy to walk through; the tree canopy blocks sunlight from the ground, so the area underneath is clear. (found in Fearon's *World Geography and Cultures*).

"Fact" 6

President Jimmy Carter was the first Democratic president of the United States to be elected to office since Harry Truman.

The True Fact: Actually, you may remember that John F. Kennedy and Lyndon B. Johnson were both presidents in the 1960s and that they were also Democrats. They were both pretty famous, too. One got his face on the half-dollar coin; one had a Texas accent.

"Fact" 7

Douglas MacArthur led the great hunt against "subversives" in the 1950s.

The True Fact: Douglas MacArthur, better known as *General* Douglas MacArthur, actually led U.S. troops in the Pacific during World War II (remember that?) and the Korean War (see *M*A*S*H*). *Joe McCarthy* was a senator who looked for subversives in America in the 1950s (from an unidentified textbook cited in the *U.S. News & World Report*).

"Fact" 8

The U.S. ended the Korean War by using the atomic bomb.

The True Fact: Actually, we didn't. We used the bomb to end World War II in Japan. We ended the Korean War by negotiating with the North Koreans. This interesting view of the war was in the textbook *American Voices,* published by Scott Foresman.

"Fact" 9

Napoleon's greatest victory was at Waterloo.

The True Fact: Close, but not quite. Yes, Napoleon was *at* Waterloo, and yes, it was his greatest something, but it was his greatest *defeat*. By modern standards, that should rate at least a C+, with two out of three correct.

Keeping Our Schools Safe

We Americans have come far from the "duck and cover" days of the early cold war when students were taught how to (theoretically) protect themselves during a nuclear attack. Now, ever-attentive school officials are on guard for new dangers and take action swiftly. We are not speaking here of terrorism but rather the hidden dangers lurking in school, unbeknownst to many, such as:

The negative psychological implications of tag

The Franklin Elementary School in Santa Monica, California, has forbidden children to play tag during recess. The ban is based upon the seemingly innocent game's dark underbelly; to wit (as explained in the school newsletter): "The running part of this activity is healthy and encouraged; however, in this game, there is a 'victim' or 'It,' which creates a self-esteem issue. The oldest or biggest child usually dominates."

The underlying threats implicit in a stick-figure drawing of a teacher

An honor-roll student at Mellon Middle School in Mount Lebanon, Pennsylvania, got a D on a vocabulary test (something she was unaccustomed to) and, to vent her anger, made a stick-figure drawing of the teacher who gave the test and a substitute teacher—both with arrows through their head. The student was suspended as the school considered the drawings "terrorist threats."

The harassment entailed in licking one's lips or teeth

This is just part of the speech code of the University of Maryland–College Park. Eager to protect its student body from sexual harassment, the school has instituted a list of forbidden behavior, including: discussing a person's clothing, body, and/or sexual activities; " 'jesting' and 'kidding' about sex or gender-specific traits"; making "suggestive or insulting sounds such as whistling, wolf-calls, or kissing sounds"; and giving out "sexually provocative compliments," "staged whispers," and "pseudo-medical advice." Other unacceptable behaviors include "licking lips or teeth" and "holding or eating food provocatively."

Stupid Zero-Tolerance Incidents in Schools

The idea is simple: To reduce the incidence of drugs and violence in American schools, institute a "zero-tolerance" policy. No more excuses, no more "simple mistakes," no more "special exceptions"—if you're guilty, out the door you go. Result: fewer problems with drugs and violent bullies at school. It sounds good, but like anything else involving rules and bureaucrats, it's now gotten absolutely ridiculous—including weird new "crimes."

Perpetrator: 5th-grade boy
Sentence: expelled for 180 days
"Crime": carrying plastic toy gun
Richard Fauble, superintendent of the Tecumseh, Michigan, school system, defended decision to expel the little plastic-toting culprit in March 2002; after national outcry, boy was allowed back in.

Perpetrator: high school honor student/top golfer
Sentence: suspended for 90 days, given failing grades for the semester

"Crime": carrying broken pocketknife

After being accused of using drugs at school (he wasn't using them), this Sandusky, Ohio, high school honor student and golfer was told to empty his pockets, where vigilant authorities found a pocketknife with a broken tip—used to clean his golfing cleats. Charged with possession of "dangerous weapon" in September 1999.

Perpetrator: 6-year-old
Sentence: suspended
"Crime": carrying plastic butter knife

This little Struthers (Ohio) Elementary School child was told he would be suspended for a "dangerous weapons violation." He allegedly took a plastic butter knife from the school cafeteria and put it in his backpack so he could take it home and show his mommy how he could butter toast all by himself. School authorities under tough-on-"crime" principal Betty Washington, apparently seeking to protect other students from illicit buttering, suspended the boy in March 2003. (In a nice twist, the boy's parents are considering a legal counterattack, suing the school for supplying the boy with a "dangerous weapon" in the first place.)

Perpetrator: 6th-grade boy
Sentence: arrested, handcuffed, fingerprinted, forced to post $250 bond
"Crime": hitting a kid back after kid insulted and hit him first

In Louisiana in 1997, this young boy was being insulted by another student; he told the student that the insults were stupid; the student then hit the boy, who responded by hitting back. Other students agreed that the 6th-grader did not instigate the fight, nor did he hit first. No matter. The young boy had violated the school rules of "nonviolent conflict resolution," and school officials resolved the conflict in their own nonviolent way: They allowed the police to arrest the 6th-grader.

Perpetrator: high school sophomore
Sentence: expelled
"Crime": bringing nail clippers to school

In 1999, a Pensacola, Florida, sophomore foolishly brought a nail clipper to school. Alert high school officials, under the supervision of principal Norm Ross, noticed that the clipper had a tiny knife (for cleaning under fingernails) and realized this violated the school's zero-tolerance policy; naturally, expulsion was in order.

Perpetrators: three 7th-graders
Sentence: sent to police station for possession of a controlled substance with intent to deliver
"Crime": possession of grape Kool-Aid

Three 7th-graders were found selling little packets of purple powder for a quarter a piece to students; they informed school officials it was merely grape Kool-Aid. Vigilant school officials were concerned it might be something more sinister; they called for police backup; students were taken to police station and rigorously interrogated; prosecutors refused to drop charges unless boys agreed to counseling. After three months, officials finally agreed to test the powder. They found it actually was . . . grape Kool-Aid.

Perpetrator: high school student
Sentence: charged under wiretap law
"Crime": tape-recording a chemistry lecture

This Navarre, Florida, student foolishly decided to tape-record a chem lecture, probably figuring it would be an easy way to check on her notes. As this was against school policy, school officials didn't bother giving her a stern reprimand; they instead filed criminal charges under the state wiretap law. Charges were eventually dropped. According to the prosecutor, "I'm not sure it's an appropriate forum for prosecution under this particular case."

Perpetrator: 11-year-old
Sentence: suspended for 10 days
"Crime": carrying Tweety bird wallet and key ring to school

A student at Garrett Middle School in Atlanta brought her Tweety bird wallet and key ring to school, unaware that the 10-inch bead-type chain that connected the key ring to the wallet was in violation of the school's weapons policy. Alert school officials nabbed the little girl and her offending Tweety bird wallet, suspended her.

Perpetrator: 9th-grader
Sentence: suspended for 10 days
"Crime": bringing throat spray and Eckerd's brand Complete Cold Relief pills to school

This student at the Port St. John Space Coast Junior/Senior High School had a cold and received permission from his father to bring some over-the-counter cold relief to school; the student didn't want to miss the last soccer match of the season. Alert school officials noticed the Eckerd's brand cold medicine and naturally suspended the boy. "This is a safety issue for the students," explained principal Larry Graves succinctly, not explaining why it was OK for students to buy and use these FDA-approved over-the-counter medicines before and after school.

Perpetrator: 13-year-old honor student/menstrual-cramp sufferer

Sentence: suspended for 10 days, agreed to attend drug-awareness program; faced expulsion

"Crime": receiving Midol from friend for menstrual cramps

A Fairborn, Ohio, honor student told a friend she had cramps. Friend proceeded to give her Midol, a mild, safe over-the-counter pain-reliever advertised on television; student receiving said substance was naturally charged by alert school officials with violating school antidrug policy; sentenced to 10 days' suspension and faced possible expulsion for using this aspirinlike painkiller at school. Fortunately, no other reports of Midol or any other illicit aspirin use have surfaced at this school since (although a school in Texas recently found and suspended another student for carrying another OTC aspirinlike substance, Advil, in her backpack).

School Sports

Ah, yes, the old school spirit as exhibited in getting out on the gridiron and winning the game for the glory of (fill in any school colors and/or team names here). But as with other educational areas, sports can be a hotbed of stupidity:

Top three stupid motivational things to do before a football game

1. Castrate a bull. According to the Associated Press, "Jackie Sherrill apologized Tuesday for allowing the castration of a bull in front of his Mississippi State Football Team.

STUDENT ORDERED TO EAT SOMEONE ELSE'S GUM

A girl caught chewing gum at Colorado City Junior High was ordered by her teacher to spit her gum into a jar containing other pieces of gum that had been chewed by other students. After the girl did this, she was told to take another of the used pieces and chew it, as punishment. The girl refused and was then ordered by officials to apologize to the teacher for refusing.

In a typical case of bureaucratic runaround, complaints about this incident were referred by Kimball Barlow, the principal, to the superintendent, Alvin Barlow, who was "not available" for comment. Mike File, the county superintendent, said helpfully that he did not have jurisdiction over discipline at schools. One can't help wondering what he does have jurisdiction over.

The bull was castrated in front of the team on a practice field before Mississippi State beat the Texas Longhorns 28–10. Later, Sherrill said he allowed the procedure because it was educational and motivational."

2. Threaten to kill celebrity students who go to the opposing team's school. Before a football game between the University of California and Stanford (then attended by President Clinton's daughter, Chelsea), the newspaper for Cal, *The Daily Californian,* wrote this "motivational" piece for the UC students: "Come, let us stream across the Bay, overtake their puny little campus and seize both the Axe and the First Daughter. . . . Any of you wishing to spread some of our rustic working-class charm to Miss Chelsea should remember that she lives in [OMITTED] dorm, and the Secret

Service guys know that killing a drunk college student would be political suicide for their boss. Show your spirit on Chelsea's bloodied carcass, because . . . she is just another student. Is hate a strong word? Yes. Is it applicable? Certainly."

3. Stage a fake shooting. In order to motivate his team for the state semifinals, Dale Christensen, an Illinois high school football coach, put on a fake shooting in front of the entire squad. It didn't work out the way he expected; in fact, later Christensen said it was a "lesson plan that went awry."

Best Innovative Cheating Before a Game

The Big Sky Conference discovered that Sacramento State players committed a "serious ethical breach." But they do deserve credit for creativity. . . . The breach? Before their game with Montana, players were trying to figure out how to avoid being tackled, and they hit on a new strategy: spraying their jerseys with the nonstick spray PAM. Not only did they get in trouble when news of the incident leaked out (aided by a photographer who caught shots of them in the act), but it wasn't enough: Sacramento lost, 31–24.

Best Way to Entertain High School Wrestlers

A high school wrestling coach managed to escape prosecution for his actions during a two-day meeting he had attended along with some assistant coaches and fifteen wrestlers. He was, however, suspended for two weeks without pay from Avon High School in Richmond, Indiana. What did he do? He bit off the head of a live bird in front of his students. According to the coach, the students "laughed and laughed." He told the Indianapolis *Star*, "They're still laughing about it. I think everyone took it as such—as innocent fun."

We Learn Faster Nowadays, So We Don't Need to Go to School as Much. . . .

Educational Advances in Elite American Colleges

	1914	1939	1964	1993
# of mandatory courses	9.9	7.3	6.9	2.5
# of courses not requiring prerequisite	23	n/a	127	582
% of colleges with thesis required for graduation	>50%	>50%	>50%	12%
days in the school year	204	195	191	156
% requiring English-composition course	99.9%	n/a	86%	36%
% requiring math	82%	n/a	36%	12%
% requiring natural science	>70%	>70%	>70%	34%
% requiring history	90%	>50%	>50%	2%
% requiring literature	75%	50%	50%	>1%

What We Can Learn in College

Here's a list of courses from 1995–2003 that weren't taught in 1914, 1939, 1964, showing how far we've advanced since then:

Philosophy and Star Trek (*Georgetown University*): The course asks "Is time travel possible?" "Is Data a person?"

Seeing Queerly: Queer Theory, Film, and Video (*Brown University*): The course asks: "While cinema has typically circumscribed vision along (heterosexually) normative lines, can film also empower viewers to see 'queerly'?"

Daytime Serials: Family and Social Roles (*University of Wisconsin*): Students analyze the "themes and characters that populate television's daytime serials."

Male Sexuality (*UC–Berkeley*): Course includes lectures by porn stars, field trips to strip clubs, visits to sex shops.

Feminist Theories of Science and Feminist Scientists (*UC–Santa Barbara*): Examines feminist critiques of science, seeks to answer the question "What is feminist science?"

Girl Culture (*Duke University*): FaT GiRLs, Cybergrrls, all-female bands. "About girlness from the 19th century to now"; "about dolls, dress-up, slumber parties, and makeovers." Includes cartoons.

Literature and Religion: Elvis Presley (*Emory University*): "In addition to music analysis, students study Pentecostal Christianity, the phenomenon of pilgrimage to Grace-land." Assignments include interviewing workers at a Burger King where Elvis was "sighted."

Magical Mushrooms, Mischievous Molds (*Cornell University*): "A light intro into the role of fungi," including athlete's foot, hallucinogenic mushrooms. Assignments include caring for pet slime mold.

CUNT FEST 2000

In November 2000, Penn State held an all-day festival called Cunt Fest. Inspired by the book *Cunt: A Declaration of Independence*, the festival celebrated the word and the organ. "Cunt originally started as a good word," explained Michelle Yates, a junior at Penn. The university was worried that some people might take the signs and flyers announcing Cunt Fest the wrong way, so the student sponsors added a bit of explanation. "If they read the flyer, they would realize no one's trying to be vulgar," said Tarah Ausburn, a senior at Penn. After all, she said, "It's time to reclaim cunt." Yates summed it all up with her somewhat utopian vision: "It would be a beautiful day for a woman to be able to say, 'Thank you. Thank you for calling me a cunt.'"

Alien Sex: Gender and Difference in Old and New Fantasy (*University of Rochester*): "Do gods, demons, incubi, androids . . . really offer a different sexuality?" Assignments include watching *Star Trek*.

The Look of the Perverse (*Tulane University*): "Examines the cultural centrality of perversion." Assignments include essays such as, "Which Is More Perverse, *Rear Window* or *Basic Instinct*?"

Soapology (*Onondaga Community College*): "The study of daytime drama." Students "critically analyze scenes, discuss soap-opera history."

Ever-So-Politically-Correct Campuses

American college campuses have long been considered hot-beds of radical thought. Think back to the '60s and campuses' role in the antiwar movement. But it is now the 21st century. That kind of radical thought is a tad *stale,* as it were—something that has become part of the mainstream.

So now college campuses are focusing on things that truly matter in this modern world: i.e., making sure things are as politically correct as possible—to the point of ridiculousness.

Names of male students are posted with sign "Notice: These Men Are Potential Rapists"

Nine female students at the University of Maryland took the names of male students picked out at random from the student directory and listed them on flyers with the headline "These Men Are Potential Rapists"—not that the men had done or were suspected of having done anything wrong. It was all to increase awareness of sexual harassment, the women said. The men were understandably angry. But "I don't think we've done anything wrong," one of the women said. "The word 'potential' was used. That's not accusatory at all."

White and colored paper renamed due to offensiveness

As part of a recycling program at Harvard Divinity School, bins for paper were placed around campus—labeled "white paper" and "colored paper." On the "colored paper" bins, someone wrote "paper of color," possibly as a joke. No matter; Harvard took it seriously and renamed the bins "bleached paper" (for white paper) and "dyed paper" (for colored paper).

Feminist Boston College professor is furious that men want the right to take her course

For 20 years, Mary Daly, a professor at Boston College, has banned men from her courses. After two men sued on the basis of discrimination in order to be allowed to take a course of hers, Daly said it was all an attack by the "patriarchy" to destroy the "rights of women and minorities so that white male power reigns."

Christmas gifts are banned at Dartmouth

In 1998, Dartmouth College in Hanover, New Hampshire, banned a campus group from giving Christmas presents through the campus mail to other students. The reason, according to Scott Brown, the dean of religion: "a large number of students would take offense." (After a load of bad publicity for the school, students were allowed to give the gifts in January.)

The word "marriage" offensive to Barnard College students

A brochure from Barnard College that stated that women at the all-female college marry and have children at a greater rate than average was denounced as "heterosexist." The college administration agreed and removed the "offensive" statement in 1998.

Ivy League college offers course in pedophilia

Cornell, in the late 1990s, offered a course entitled "The Sexual Child," in which propedophilia (child-porn) readings were required, as was looking at photos of nude children. One reading compared boy lovers to harassed communists and gay people in the 1950s. The professor of this course, Ellis Hanson, feels that erotic fascination with children is so prevalent that we feel compelled to "accept, study, and celebrate it."

Enlightened Education Funding in the Big Apple

It's the prime example of spending education money where it *really* matters:

On chauffeured cars, of course.

More specifically, New York City schools chancellor Joel Klein rides in a chauffeured limo while poor school kids under his administration go without lunch aides.

It sounds almost like a scene from a Dickens novel. Because of a budget crisis, New York City recently announced it was laying off 3,200 lunch and teacher's aides to save money. Meanwhile, it is continuing to give its Board

CLASS TRIP TO SEE CHARLES DICKENS'S *A CHRISTMAS CAROL* IS CANCELED DUE TO OFFENSE IT MAY CAUSE OTHERS

In Christmas 2002, the 6th-grade class of South Orange Middle School in New Jersey were all set to go to see the traditional Dickens classic *A Christmas Carol* when the outing was suddenly canceled. Apparently, some parents complained that the show had something to do with Christmas. Students went to see *The Great Railroad Race* instead.

★

THE WONDERFUL WORD OF MAKE-BELIEVE
AFRICAN-AMERICAN STUDENTS

Worried that their catalog didn't express the incredible diversity on the campus, University of Wisconsin administrators used a bit of computer retouching to add a black student to the cover of a brochure, to project an image of diversity. Two weeks later, it was discovered that the University of Idaho did similar retouching—a picture of nine students on their website had been changed, with the heads of two white students replaced by two black ones. (They removed the picture from the site.)

of Education head honchos chauffeured cars along with bodyguard/drivers. (Why can't they take cabs or the subway like everyone else? And do they really need bodyguards? one might ask. It's unlikely you'll get an answer. . . .) The cars even come equipped with *sirens.* The New York *Daily News* recently spotted a driver for $250,000-a-year Deputy Chancellor Diana Lam "shoo[ing] another car away with lights and sirens"—despite a City Hall directive that says sirens should be used only in emergencies. The *Daily News* also spotted another Board of Ed honcho, Deputy Chancellor Anthony Shorris (who takes home $168,700), taking his son to school in a chauffeured city car. Chancellor Klein himself has two drivers assigned to him. In total, the *Daily News* estimates these vital perks cost at least $580,000 a year—enough to pay the salaries of twenty-eight school aides. But priorities are priorities. . . .

According to the Plano, Texas, Unofficial School webpage, Harrington Elementary School posted photographs of prominent black Americans—including one of O. J. Simpson.

Great Discoveries by Modern American Academics

OK—who and what comes out of the American educational system? Sometimes great things and great thinkers: DNA, courtesy Watson and Crick (and some other people who didn't get as much publicity); computers; transistors; literature; and . . . well, many other things.

But then we come to the social sciences—the study of human beings in society—which is often seen as the poor cousin of "hard" sciences like physics, chemistry, and biology. Scientists of the "hard sciences" discover exotic chemical compounds, save lives, rake in millions, remake our images of reality. Given all this sexy science, can social scientists also make their contributions to the world? Of *course* they can, as these electrifying discoveries by top American social scientists show:

War can cause stress and frighten children.

> —surprising conclusions reported on the front page of the *Journal of the American Academy of Pediatrics*

The loss of hope is . . . a stronger sign that a person may commit suicide than other factors.

> —astonishing discovery made by a University of Kansas researcher, reported in the science section of *The New York Times*

Cool pose [of poor urban blacks] is a bit of posturing that insulates them from an otherwise overwhelming social reality.

> —amazing find reported in *The New York Times;* it took a team of researchers six years to discover this

Happy or Sad, a Mood Can Prove Contagious.

> —shocking discovery by Dr. John Cacciopo, who also found that "the more emotionally expressive people are, the more apt they are to transmit their moods." Reported in *The New Republic*

Anger, Stopping Smoking and Loud Noises Produce Jaw-clenching in Humans.

> —stunning finding made by the National Science Foundation and the Office of Naval Research, after spending more than $500,000

Popping bubble wrap makes people calmer.

> —amazing discovery by Dr. Kathleen Dillon found that people who pop bubble wrap experience a significant increase in energy when doing the popping, followed by calming feeling

People function better on a "psycho-social scale" after their teeth are fixed by orthodontists.

> —unexpected conclusion after a $465,500 study by the U.S. government–funded National Institute of Dental Research

Those Wacky Baby-Killing* Professors

Maybe there's something in the water on certain college campuses. But recently, at three separate campuses, three different professors came up with variations on the same bizarre idea.

University of Colorado professor says new moms should get a week to kill their kids

How can happiness in society be increased? Consider killing a baby. Michael Tooley of the University of Colorado says there "should be some period of time, such as a week after birth, as the interval during which infanticide will be permitted." He feels that if moral objections to infanticide were removed, "the happiness of society could be significantly improved."

MIT professor says it's OK for new moms to kill babies if they don't want to have a baby after all

Speaking in the wake of the famous killer-nanny trial in Boston, MIT professor Steven Pinker explained that its actually OK to kill a baby, since "babies aren't real people because they don't have an ability to reflect upon themselves." He goes on to suggest that "a new mother should first coolly assess the infant and her situation" and then decide whether to kill or not.

*(advocating)

Princeton professor Peter Singer: Kill deformed babies for their own good

This academic favors killing deformed babies because he knows that they will grow up to be unhappier than other people. However, he is against killing animals; as a vegetarian, he says, "It is speciesist to judge that the life of a normal adult member of our species is more valuable than the life of a normal adult mouse." (He has also denounced consumer society, championing his own nonmaterialist lifestyle on the Princeton campus as an example. What he does not note is that not all of us are entitled to free access to the fine Princeton gymnasiums, swimming pools, libraries, and other upper-class facilities, which he receives free and for which the university charges students more than $30,000 a year.)

Stupid Government and Bureaucracy in the U.S.A.

The U.S. government—and all other official and quasi-official bureaucracies—is the source of much material on the stupid side of things. Perhaps this surprises you. Perhaps you think, as a red-blooded patriot, that it is impossible for the government (whether federal, state, or municipal) to do anything stupid . . . and for our elected or appointed officials to do anything stupid. (Perhaps you also haven't been reading the papers, watching television news, or keeping up with current events. But that is none of our business.)

We will not argue with you. Instead, we would like to politely direct your attention to the information that follows.

Great Moments in Enlightened Self-interest for Our Public Servants

People who work for the city, state, and federal governments are often called "public servants." The idea is that they serve the public selflessly; they set aside the chance for big money—say the $189 million Derek Jeter of the New York Yankees is getting—and instead settle for lower government salaries and benefits and per diems and mandatory in-step pay raises and job security and performance bonuses and rock-solid retirement packages. . . . But for some, this is not enough.

Let us acknowledge those who just want a little more and have the guts to go out and get it (even if it is sometimes just a mite unethical):

- **Presidential and Pentagon adviser Richard Perle,** who has raised the notion of "hairsplitting" to a fine art:

  Technically not an official government employee, he's instead termed a "special government employee"—and he has gotten some "special" money. More to the point, he served as chairman of the Defense Policy Board, a group that advises Defense Secretary Donald Rumsfeld, *and* just happens to also be involved with telecom company Global Crossing, which wanted to get government approval for selling its fiber-optic network to two Asian firms. For helping Global Crossing, Perle was due to receive a cool $725,000. Some felt this was a possible conflict of interest, and a government group reviewed the deal. Confronted with keeping the money or keeping his job title as a very special servant of the public, Perle took the principled high road: He took the money. A man of "integrity and honor," to quote Rumsfeld, Perle resigned the *chairmanship* of the government advisory group and kept his chance for the big money. He, however, continues to serve on the board itself.

- *Illinois state assemblyman Roger P. McAuliffe,* who has mastered the art of legislation . . . when it comes to self-betterment.

  Former police officer and current assemblyman Roger P. McAuliffe of Chicago introduced a special bill in 1995 making all former police officers now serving as state assemblymen eligible to receive pensions from both workplaces. The bill was passed and signed by Governor James Edgar. Total number of statewide beneficiaries of this bill? One: former police officer and current assemblyman Roger P. McAuliffe.

- *52-year-old state employee John Orabona,* who managed to snag a government pension based on *79* years of service.

  Orabona claimed a pension based on 79 years of state employment, for a total of $106,000 per year. How can a man 52 years old get credit for 79 years of work? There's a quirk in the state law, involving getting credit for different jobs done at the same time. This was due to special legislation voted on by one special man: 52-year-old John Orabona.

- *Quasi-government official William J. Catocosinos,* who ran a public utility into the ground and simultaneously grabbed a healthy $42 million as a severance package.

  Catocosinos was CEO of New York–based Long Island Lighting Company (LILCO), which had a history of putting the thumbscrews on its customers by charging them the highest electric rates in the country. In May 1998, LILCO was taken over by a special state public-benefit corporation, the Long Island Power Authority. Catocosinos was taking a job with the new corporation— but also happened to push through a hefty severance package of $42 million . . . which, as one might expect, wasn't clearly disclosed to shareholders, wasn't mentioned to the board of directors, and was rather obfuscated. The one bright note: LILCO customers weren't charged for the compensation. Though, of course, Catocosinos got to keep the money.

- *Democratic National Committee chairman Terry McAuliffe,* who managed to turn a cool $18 million profit on a $100,000 investment.

Few of us have the marketing timing and the investment strategy to turn an 18,000% profit in less than a year and a half. McAuliffe, apparently, is one of those special few. Quick to make a hue and cry when Enron filed for bankruptcy, he was not *quite* so bellicose when it came to the investigation of Global Crossing's accounting practices. Perhaps this is because he traded (profitably) Global Crossing stocks and options? Oh, and he did some "political work" for the CEO as well, setting up a golf meeting for him with President Clinton. What did they get in return? Clinton got a $1 million contribution to his library fund. Global Crossing got a $400 million Pentagon contract (which was later canceled by the Bush administration). McAuliffe didn't get anything—other than the $18 million, which he garnered through sheer investor shrewdness, we can only surmise . . .

JIM MCGREEVY: THE PEOPLE'S GOVERNOR

Our nomination for "The People's Governor": governor of New Jersey Jim McGreevey, for the following meritorious actions:

- Suggested that state workers work for 90 days without pay to save the state money. Didn't seem to offer much in the way of cutting his own pay, however.

- Delayed moving into the governor's mansion because his wife wanted it renovated, and he didn't want to spend his own money. Asked for donations: "Dina [his wife] is soliciting paint, tiles and wallpaper."

- Uses State Police helicopter for quick (and expensive) trips. The governor's office said he "always intended to reimburse the state at the end of the year." At the end of 2002, the state Democratic Committee agreed to pick up the tab for 14 political and personal trips—to the tune of $1,200 per trip.

- Went on a trade mission to Ireland, which he predicted would cost taxpayers $20,000. He was wrong. It cost $105,000—perhaps due to the Mercedes that chauffeured him, the first-class plane trip, or the luxury hotels at which he stayed. The day he left for Ireland he released the $20,000 figure but had already spent $36,000. The trip failed to result in any trade agreements or business deals.

- Although laying off 1,200 workers due to a state budget crisis, gave himself a large raise to $154,000, in addition to free housing, transportation, and so on.

- During the same budget crisis, hired at $110,000 per year Golan Cipil, a reporter and poet whose chief qualification was that he was an Israeli naval reservist, as the director of the state's newly created security agency, despite the fact that ex–FBI head Louis Freeh offered to do the job for free. After a public outcry, replaced Cipil—he now put him in as a "policy analyst"—at $110,000 a year, for doing essentially nothing.

- At first nominated as state police chief an officer previously arrested for assaulting another officer, as well as once being charged with income-tax evasion.

- Approved another (there's already one) multimillion-dollar arena in Camden County—of direct benefit to a local Democratic bigwig. Twenty-four million dollars is to be "invested" by the state out of tax dollars to help this bigwig friend, but taxpayers are not allowed to vote on the issue.

- Hammered away during his campaign at how badly his opponent had managed the budget while governor. Finally, a reporter asked him how *he* would manage the budget. McGreevey looked dumbfounded. He was silent for a moment, then stammered and finally in a panic mumbled that he had to "probably refer" the reporter to the Democratic spokesman on fiscal issues.

Fun Congressional Facts

Let us now turn our eye on a different group: those who serve the public in Congress.

We are, of course, not putting forth the idea that our esteemed public servants, those men and women who put aside personal gain to toil as representatives or senators, are stupid.

Far from it.

What might be construed as stupid is the fact that we, the public, call these people "servants." A few salient facts:

- Percentage of representatives and senators who are millionaires: 25%

Percentage of freshmen congressmen elected in 2002 who are millionaires: 43% (27 out of 63)

Percentage of U.S. population who are millionaires: 1%

- Monthly pension paid to anyone who has served in Congress for any period of time: more than $15,000

Total pension paid to most representatives and senators: more than $1 million

Total pension paid to long-tenured representatives and senators: more than $7 million

Total cash contributions to pension by representatives and senators: zero

- Salary paid to senators and representatives: between $154,700 and $192,100

Salary paid to senators and representatives in founding years of republic: $6 a day for each day in session ($119 in today's dollars)

- Amount congressional salaries have gone up since 1999: $18,000

Percentage congressional salaries have increased over eight years: 16%

Total monetary amount in raises members of Congress have granted themselves from 1989 to 2002: $60,500 (http://www.counterpunch.org/nader0824.html)

Hourly minimum wage that Congress has frozen for six years: $5.15

Median income of American families in 2000: $43,100

Median income of American families in 2001: $42,148

- Justification given for voting for a congressional pay raise shortly after 9/11: It was a "national security measure"

- Time at which vote on a congressional pay raise was held in 2002: 10:30 P.M.

- Additional moneys members of Congress can earn from public speaking, legal practice, consulting: 15% of their federal salary

  Additional moneys members of Congress can earn from book royalties: unlimited

- Ratio of lawyers in the House to lawyers in the voting-age population: 38 to 1

  Ratio of House members with real estate, insurance, and finance backgrounds to ordinary citizens with those backgrounds: 4 to 1. (Center for Voting and Democracy, 1998)

- Monthly premium for individual coverage under the congressional health insurance plan: $73.04

  Average monthly premium for individual HMO coverage in the U.S.: $212.71 (as of 2002; expected to increase by about 18% in 2003)

  Percentage of congressional insurance premium paid for by taxpayers: 72% of "program-wide weighted average of premiums in effect each year" or 75% of the "total premium for the particular plan an enrollee selects"

Annual fee members of Congress pay to use Attending Physician's Office medical facilities (which include 20 doctors, nurses, and technicians in three separate facilities): $332 for House members, $520 for senators

Annual taxpayer subsidy for Attending Physician: about $1.6 million

• Annual cost for members of Congress to use the Senate or House health clubs: $400

Number of physical therapists on staff at health clubs: 11

Amenities of those health clubs: swimming pools, saunas, steam baths, bodybuilding and exercise equipment, whirlpools, heated pool, and more

Daily number of hours Senate and House health clubs are open: 16

Just Plain Folks:
When Politicians Try to Act Like You and Me

Often, in efforts to garner votes or support, politicians pretend that they're not millionaires or Washington insiders but regular Joes. The kind of person who shops at Wal-Mart, needs his tax refund to buy a new couch, and so on. Clearly, politicians feel that John or Jane Q. Voter will think, "Gee. He or she is not a wealthy Washington insider who could buy and sell my entire neighborhood. He's just plain folks." However, all too often, this thought never occurs to

WHAT PEOPLE KNOW ABOUT
THE U.S. SYSTEM OF GOVERNMENT

Perhaps we get what we deserve. . . . According to two different surveys, one conducted by the National Constitutional Center in September 1997 and another commissioned by Columbia Law School in May 2002:

- One of the rights guaranteed by the First Amendment is "freedom from fear"

- The first ten amendments are called "the Pledge of Allegiance"

- Norman Schwarzkopf is the commander-in-chief

- Karl Marx's famous saying "From each according to his ability, to each according to his needs" either was, or may have been, included in the Constitution. (This was thought by nearly two thirds of those polled)

said John or Jane as this time-honored campaign trick has a fascinating tendency to backfire. . . .

Best Fast-Food Moment

Counterperson at McDonald's: "What do you want to drink?"

James Buckley (R–New York), wealthy candidate for senator: "What's your house Chablis?"

Best Overprepared Moment (or, How many people can answer this for more than one state?)

Man in Connecticut supermarket: "Do you know the price of milk?"

Steve Forbes, wealthy Republican candidate for president: "A dollar eighty-nine here, and $2.69 in New Jersey. It's $1.99 in New Hampshire."

Best Existential Moment (or, It's not money; I just get high on life)

"I do believe in smelling the flowers. Occasionally, I will take my staff out to the lawn out there and sit there and say, 'Look at this Capitol, look at these trees. Smell it."

> —Michael Huffington, who spent $28 million in an attempt to win a California senate seat

Best Back-to-the-Land Moment

"I'm very familiar with the importance of dairy farming in Wisconsin. I've spent the night on a dairy farm here in Wisconsin. If I'm entrusted with the presidency, you'll have someone who is very familiar with what the Wisconsin dairy industry is all about."

> —Al Gore to Wisconsin dairy farmers

Best Overidentification Moment

"I wish I were a Jew."

> —Senator John D. Rockefeller IV (D–West Virginia), closing a speech at the American Israel Public Affairs Committee

Dirty Rotten Scoundrels; or, Elected Officials: The "I Am Not a Crook" Awards

As unbelievable as it may sound, some elected officials don't always tell the truth—even when campaign season is over. But some politicians are more brazen (or more un-lucky) than others when it comes to being caught. Here are a few of the best examples of American white-collar crime, political-style—truly award-winning moments in politics.

Best Excuse (Local): Washington state senator Joe Zarelli (R)

Zarelli had collected $12,000 in unemployment benefits for 2001–2002 and neglected to mention that he was also get-ting a salary: $32,000 a year as a state senator. When this discrepancy was pointed out to him during an interview with *The Columbian* newspaper, he explained that he "had no clue" that he was supposed to report his salary. He also commented that it was actually the state bureaucracy at fault for not catching him and explaining to him that he shouldn't have done it. And, he added, he felt the only rea-son the Employment Security Agency was after him was be-cause he was a Republican.

Best Excuse (Municipal): New York City mayor David Dinkins (D)

When accused of failing to pay income taxes from 1969 to 1972, Dinkins found it the perfect moment to split hairs by explaining (none too helpfully): "I haven't committed a crime. What I did was fail to comply with the law." He also added that paying taxes "was one of the things I was always going to take care of, but sometimes I did not have all the funds available or I did not have all the documents or other materials I needed." (He did eventually pay the back taxes, plus penalties and interest.)

Most Mind-boggling Resignation Speech:
Senator Robert Torricelli (D–New Jersey)

Torricelli was severely admonished by the Senate ethics committee for accepting gifts from political donor/businessman David Chang, who, coincidentally, received aid from the senator in his business ventures in North and South Korea. The gifts included: a television set, a CD player, earrings (for Torricelli's sister, friend, and employee), and a "loan" of bronze statues of an eagle and a broncobuster, which Torricelli displayed in his office. While initially hoping to continue in his race to retain his Senate seat, Torricelli finally resigned—and in grand style. In his speech, he first took the "it's not my fault, it's America's fault" tack:

> *I am a human being, and while I have not done the things that I have been accused of doing, I most certainly have made mistakes. There will be those who have concluded that those mistakes bring justice to this moment because there's a price to be paid. When did we become such an unforgiving people? How did we become a society when a person can build credibility your entire life to have it questioned by someone whose word is of no value at all? When did we stop believing in and trusting in each other? I remember an America where, when a person made an error and they asked forgiveness, it was given.*

Then he went for the heartstrings with a harking back to his youth—and his desire to serve the public (with no mention of receiving gifts for said service):

> *In a foolish moment in my life, when I was no more than 5 or 6, my mother entered my room one day, and I was writ-*

ing out my will. She said, "Robert, why are you doing this? And whoever are you leaving your things to?" I left the only things I ever owned—I wrote on it—I wrote on it, "To the United States Marine Corps"—because that's where my father had served—"and to my country."

Career Achievement Award (State Division): Georgia state senator Ralph David Abernathy III (D)

Abernathy announced his retirement from politics in 1998 after his reelection filing-fee check of $400 bounced. Among the highlights of his career: He followed a woman into a state-capitol ladies' room; was caught with marijuana in his underwear at the Atlanta airport; was sent to prison for theft for taking $5,700 in state funds and violating his oath of office; and was accused of taking $35,000 from two women after promising to win the release of their loved ones from prison. While in his retirement announcement he said he planned to enter the seminary, instead he was headed for prison yet again—after being convicted on parole violations.

Career Achievement Award (Federal Division): Representative Corrine Brown (D-Florida)

Brown wins this award for the breadth of her accomplishments. Among them: She failed to pay employment taxes to Florida; was sued for unpaid bills by several airlines and Whirlpool; failed to report the sale of her travel agency; owed $14,228 in back taxes; was investigated by House ethics committee for possible bribe taking; refused to file conflict-of-interest reports to the House involving her travel agency and the airlines she oversaw; charged with money laundering.

Most Creative Résumé Embellishment:
Representative Wes Cooley (R-Oregon)

Cooley has a history of *colorful* comments on his background—which, under scrutiny, just don't seem to hold water. (Perhaps this is why he wasn't reelected?) He claimed he served in Special Operations in Korea—but it was found that he never served in Korea and actually finished basic training after the war had ended. (He later said that he hadn't meant to imply that he was actually *in* Korea but rather that he served *during* the Korean War.) He also claimed that he was a world-class motorcycle racer and was once ranked ninth in the world. (According to records kept by official world motorcycling groups, this is not the case.) His wife also got into the family game—she and her husband allegedly concealed their marriage so she could continue collecting veteran's survivor's benefits as the widow of a Marine.

Best Reason for Admission of Guilt (or, "We didn't do it but don't have the money to prove it"):
Senator Jesse Helms (R-North Carolina)

The Jesse Helms campaign, the North Carolina Republican Party, and four political consulting/marketing firms were charged with violations of the Voting Rights Act in 1990 because they sent out 125,000 postcards headlined "Voter Registration Bulletins," chiefly to African-American voters. The cards said that the recipients might not be able to vote and that they would be prosecuted for fraud if they did vote. It was a tight race, but Helms won. In 1992, the Justice Department ruled against such mailings . . . but it was a bit too late. The Helms campaign signed an admission of guilt, explaining later that they weren't really guilty but simply lacked the funds to fight the allegation in court. (Helms and his campaign staffers were not prosecuted.)

Best Insanity Defense: Former Representative Edward Mezvinsky (D-Iowa)

Clinton buddy Mezvinsky was indicted in March 2001 on 66 counts of defrauding banks and individuals (including friends, business associates, and family—including his mother-in-law) of more than $10 million. Chief among his activities: being party to what are called "Nigerian advance-fee schemes," in which con artists pose as African royalty or aides to royalty and promise the recipient of the letter or e-mail a great deal of money . . . *if* the person first puts up a small percentage of money as a fee or other cost. He claimed insanity: He was bipolar and was taking a malaria drug, Lariam, which made him even *more* crazy. Said his attorney: "The drug made him worse—he didn't know he was crazy—and as a person suffering from bipolar disorder he didn't see the downside to these bizarre financial investments." He was sentenced to 6½ years.

Stupid Congress

It seems that Congress has its priorities in order: Avoid controversy at all costs. Just before the Iraq war, as people were angrily debating it, and just as North Korea was apparently gearing up its nuclear reactors, and just as Iran was found to have an advanced reactor, and just as the Serbian prime minister was assassinated, and just as the U.S. stock market was tanking—what was our Congress doing? Weighing in on the conflicts of the day?

Of course not.

All of that would be too controversial. It could even cause an intrepid politician to lose a few votes.

Instead, Congress was busily debating human *cloning*, which, according to polls, an overwhelming majority of American citizens were against—besides which, according to most reputable scientists, no one could clone a human yet anyway. That didn't bother Congress: Just in case we survived all those other problems, and just in case we developed human cloning a little early, they decided to announce their opposition to it. A very useful organization, Congress. . . .

Some other wonderfully useless bits of congressional legislation or doings:

Congress announces only big olives for our boys overseas

Senator Vic Fazio (D–California) snuck a vital measure into the defense appropriation bill; by law, the Defense Department may purchase only *large-sized* olives for soldiers.

Senate approves $230,000 to confront a pressing threat: chicken shit in Oklahoma

Senator Tom Daschle (D–South Dakota), always ready to weigh in on the truly controversial matters that face our nation, said it best in supporting this piece of vital legislation: "Poultry waste . . . is something that continues to threaten our country."

Congress denounces French fries (and French toast, too!)

Ohio Republican representative Bob Ney, whose committee was in charge of House cafeterias, announced a "small but symbolic effort": French fries would hereby be known as "freedom fries" and French toast as "freedom toast," due to French opposition to the Iraq war. Jose Serrano (D–New York) called this act "petty grandstanding" and suggested Congress get back to more pressing matters . . . such as the faltering economy.

Congressman orders nudie statue removed

Representative Edward Roybal (D–California), visiting the Edward R. Roybal Center and Federal Building in Los Angeles (yes, it's named after him), spied a statue of a nude woman holding a baby in her arms. He at once ordered the statue removed because it would "attract the homeless, . . . perverts, and graffiti artists."

Congress approves a $100,000 grant for "Weed It Now!"

Tired of weeds in western Massachusetts? Congress knew that this is an issue dear to many American hearts and approved a grant to help defray the cost of weed pulling in the Berkshire Mountains, courtesy of American taxpayers.

Congress stands for clean water . . . and clean water . . . and clean water (repeat this 70 more times)

According to the Citizens for a Sound Economy Issues Analysis, as of April 2, 1999, Congress has authorized 74 different clean-water programs, 127 programs for at-risk youth, 340 programs for children and families, 64 economic-development programs, and 12 food-safety programs.

SENATOR JOHN KERRY (D–MASSACHUSETTS), EVERYONE'S CANDIDATE!!

Kerry, who in 2002 voted for use of force against Iraq, campaigned as an antiwar candidate in 2003. Why aren't we surprised?

January 22, 1991, Letter to a Constituent
Thank you for contacting me to express your opposition . . . to the early use of military by the US against Iraq. I share your concerns. On January 11, I voted for a resolution that would have insisted that economic sanctions be given more time to work and against a resolution giving the president the immediate authority to go to war.

January 31, 1991, Letter to the *Same* Constituent
Thank you for contacting me to express your support for the actions of President Bush in response to the Iraqi invasion of Kuwait. From the outset of the invasion, I have strongly and unequivocally supported President Bush's response to the crises and the policy goals he has established with our military deployment in the Persian Gulf.

Brilliance in Bureaucracy

The American musical *South Pacific* sagely noted that there is "nothing like a dame."

In these more enlightened times (in which terms like "dame" are no longer used for fear of retribution by lawyer Gloria Allred and her ilk), we would like to paraphrase:

There is nothing like a bureaucrat.

Indeed there is not. Every country boasts bureaucrats, but we like to think ethnocentrically, if we may: American bureaucrats push the envelope.

Let us pause here to acknowledge the U.S. Tax Code—

NATIONAL DEATH ZOO

In the past few years, Keltie the gray seal, Nancy the African elephant, Tana the lion, Bikita the cheetah, Taj the white tiger, Ryma and Griff the giraffes, Kiska the brown bear, Pensi the orangutan, Hsing-Hsing the giant panda, as well as two red pandas, a pygmy hippo, a bobcat, and two zebras all died under somewhat . . . mysterious . . . circumstances under the reign of Lucy Spelman, chief veterinarian and now director of the National Zoo. Besides being in charge of the dead animals, Spelman has been instrumental in carrying out the Smithsonian's plan to abolish the world-famous research facility at the zoo in favor of more "popular" and money-raising exhibits; one exhibit will be sponsored by Fujifilm. But back to the animals. Why did so many animals die in so short a time? According to Spelman, the deaths were for various reasons, including natural causes. According to others, they involved feeding them rat poison by mistake, starving some by mistake, and so on.

In light of the controversy, could Spelman show reporters and the public the records of how the animals died? No. Why not? According to Spelman, one reason has to do with that good old American virtue: principle.

Wrote *The Washington Post:* "The Smithsonian Institution's National Zoo has taken the position that viewing animal records would violate the animal's rights to privacy and be an intrusion into the zookeeper-animal relationship."

all 2.8 million words of it. Thank you. And now let us acknowledge *other* examples of bungled (or, rather, brilliant) bureaucracy in action:

16 people needed to change lightbulb at Rocky Flats U.S. government plant

How many workers are needed to change a lightbulb in Golden, Colorado? 16. According to a memo written by a manager at the U.S. Department of Energy, 16 people should take about 60 hours to replace the "criticality beacon" (a flashing red light like a police light) at the nuclear plant. The memo called for current workers to meet with other workers who had done the job before, obtain approval signatures from coworkers, get the work-project plans approved by various officials—then direct the electricians to put in the bulb. Total time: 60 hours; total manpower, 16 workers. (Previously, it had taken "only" 4.15 hours and 12 employees.)

Classified document from 1917 locked in Army safe and declassified only in 1992

From the *Chicago Tribune*:

> *A file designated WCD-9944-X-1 lies under lock and key on the sixth floor of the National Archives. Inside the file, faded and frail with age, is the oldest classified document in the United States. Subject: troop movements in Europe. Date: April 15, 1917—nine days after the United States entered World War I. Classification: Confidential. The document stays secret because the US Army says releasing it would damage national security. Finally, in 1992, the government deemed it was safe to release the information to the public.*

NASA surprised that no one volunteered to have jet-engine noise blasted into their homes for 14 hours a day

NASA proposed an experiment involving the broadcasting of jet-aircraft noise into people's homes for 14 hours a day, in order to test their reactions. Surprisingly, there were no volunteers.

Florida Department of Children and Families can't find 500 kids under its care

The Florida Department of Children and Families (DCF) admitted in 2002 that it couldn't find 532 children under its supervision. "We can't be perfect" seemed to be the basic excuse. According to Jack Moss, a district administrator, the problem was simple: "We have a fixed amount of assets." So a local paper, the *Sun-Sentinel,* decided to give it a try itself. It took cases involving 24 missing children in their local area and found more than one third of the "missing" children in four weeks. Four were found within one mile of the DCF offices. One kid was found at an address that was in the DCF files. One kid was found after a few minutes by calling two of his relatives. (The DCF had listed him as having been missing for eight years.) After the children had been found by the newspaper, the DCF issued a statement that "appropriate actions had already, in fact, been taken and the locations of the children [were] known to DCF personnel."

Elevator inspectors required for towns with no elevators

Three New Jersey townships—Upper Pittsgrove, Alloway, and Quinton—in 1993 contracted for elevator inspectors, as per the orders of the state Department of Community Affairs (DCA). One problem: There are no elevators in any of the three towns. That's no excuse, according to a DCA spokesman. The towns have to get and pay for inspectors, "otherwise, the Uniform Construction Code would no longer be uniform."

Department of Agriculture doesn't know how big it is

When a Senate agriculture committee staffer requested information from the Department of Agriculture as to the "size and whereabouts of the department's staff in Washington and across the nation," he was told it just didn't know. Two months after the request, he received a memo from the USDA stating, "You asked for the number of local USDA offices around the country. We have tried to get a straight answer to this question for as long as I have been here. Our staff still cannot give us an accurate number."

1,012-page state bill passed—to reduce paperwork

In 1995, Missouri state legislators approved a 1,012-page bill, weighing in at five pounds—to reduce paperwork in the state.

Wildlife Service authorizes Air Force bombing in wildlife refuge

The U.S. Fish and Wildlife Service agreed to let the Air Force use about 75% of the Desert National Wildlife Refuge for bombing runs and exercises. According to a spokesman for the Wildlife Service, "We feel the animals are in safe hands."

U.S. military computer not warlike enough

A computer system programmed by the RAND Corporation to help U.S. military leaders simulate international conflicts kept concluding that escalation to war was irrational. So, according to *Federal Computer Week* magazine, the Pentagon did the rational thing: They ordered RAND to reprogram the computer to declare war more often.

Bonus given to creator of the visa program that allowed 9/11 terrorists to enter the country with expedited visas

The State Department awarded an "outstanding performance" bonus of $15,000 to Mary Ryan, the head of the office that devised the "visa express" program that allowed 13 of the 19 9/11 hijackers to enter the country with expedited visas. Ryan received the award for the 12-month period beginning April 2001—which encompassed 9/11.

FBI gives "exceptional performance" award to head of FBI office that didn't follow up an investigation of so-called 20th terrorist

The FBI gave an "exceptional performance" award (and a bonus of more than $10,000) to FBI official Marion "Spike" Bowman, for work over a period including 9/11. Bowman heads up the Minneapolis FBI office—the one that came under scrutiny after FBI agent Colleen Rowley blew the whistle on it, saying that it didn't follow up on investigating Zacaraias Moussaoui (also known as the 20th terrorist).

A BRILLIANT BUREAUCRATIC EXCUSE

In 2001, the U.S. Navy was hauled into court for using a tiny Pacific Island as a bombing target and in the process killing thousands of birds. This violated the Migratory Bird Treaty Act, but the Navy had its good excuse for killing birds: It was actually *helping* bird-watchers. As the Navy lawyer told the judge: "In some respects, bird-watchers get more enjoyment spotting a rare bird than they do a common one."

TIME MARCHES ON. . . .

Number of pages of U.S. Tariff Code in 1790: 1
Number of pages of U.S. Tariff Code in 1993: 8,757

Doggie Ethics

Two bloodhounds in West Virginia were banned from the making of a television commercial for Buckeye Feed, which gives them their dog food for free. The problem? The dogs work at the State Forestry Division, investigating forest fires. The Forestry Division hoped that by appearing in the ads, the dogs would increase public awareness of the agency's bloodhound program. But according to the state ethics commission, the dogs are state employees. State employees are not allowed to use their public positions for monetary awards.

Superbig Late Fees

Robert Challender of Reno, showing up a month late to register his 1978 Datsun, received a late-fee bill for $378,426.25 from the Nevada Department of Motor Vehicles, of which $260,000 were for penalties. The DMV explained he was mistakenly charged for late fees dating back to 1900, before there were any cars at all in Nevada, especially 1978 Datsuns.

How to Lose an Election

Perhaps you are now thinking, "I, *too*, should become a public servant, work on important legislation, and get happy perks and pay." Here are some tips on what *not* to do should you want to win an election, from candidates who lost their particular races:

Tip #1: Write "nudie" films

Harold Gunn of Houston was running for state representative. He got ousted in the Republican primary because of a different type of running. . . . Voters learned that in 1983 he wrote and appeared in a film that revolved around a nude woman jogging and another in which he (nude) covered his body with motor oil. The latter film was called, most appropriately, *The Great Texas Showoff*. Explaining how the films do not violate what the Republican Party stands for, Gunn said, "It's no big deal. It just shows I am a great communicator." About the movies themselves, they're "not pornography. There is no sex and no dirty language. It's as tasteful as it can get with naked women in it."

Tip #2: Urinate in a voter's yard

Mike Rucker, candidate for county commissioner in Tallahassee, Florida, urinated in a voter's yard moments after the voter said he wouldn't post Rucker's campaign sign. Rucker apologized, claiming it had nothing to do with the sign but rather was due to a prostate problem.

Tip #3: Bludgeon and butcher a goat in a vacant lot

The *Bay Area Reporter* ran a story about San Francisco city-supervisor candidate Makinka Moye. He had been arrested earlier that year for bludgeoning and butchering a goat on a vacant lot near a city recreation center.

Tip #4: Brag on tape that you had sex in your office with five women

An audiotape of Joe Paulus, district attorney in Oshkosh, Wisconsin, circulated when he was running in the primary. On the tape, he was heard boasting that he had had sex with five different women in his office. Paulus claimed it was mere "boy talk" while out with the guys—but the voters apparently were unimpressed by his excuse and he lost his bid for reelection.

Tip #5: If male, wear a dress while in an "adult" bookstore—and shoot and kill the purse snatcher who takes your purse

Robert Bouslaugh was running for sheriff in La Plata County, Colorado, and happened to be in drag in an adult bookstore when a man stole his purse. Bouslaugh shot and killed the snatcher . . . and later explained that he was a retired law-enforcement officer (he wouldn't say from where, though) and was in the dress as he was "working undercover." He did not, however, supply any more details about his undercover assignment.

Tip #6: If running for governor, claim to already be in charge—for life—and have as your slogan the catchy "I'm the damn governor. I'm running the damn state"

Aneb Jah Rasta Sensas-Utcha Nefer I was the Rasta Movement candidate for Wisconsin governor—although he said he had already been elected governor before birth.

Tip #7: Spit on the talk-show host who is interviewing you

California's libertarian candidate for governor Gary Copeland got annoyed with KABC talk-show host Mark Whitman when Whitman turned off Copeland's mike. So he spit on him. After Copeland came clean in *The Orange County Register,* the Libertarian Party met to discuss dropping him as their candidate.

Tip #8: Shoot at your opponent's house

In Florida, Seminole County Democrat Eric Adam Kaplan was criticized by his fellow Democrats for running a dull campaign in this heavily Republican county. Kaplan apparently decided that shooting off a gun would give his campaign the jump start it needed. He fired five shots into the home of his opponent, hitting his opponent's wife's leg in the process. He was arrested. "We believe he wanted to win in the worst way," said the local sheriff.

Political Supporters; or, "With Friends Like These ..."

Politics makes strange bedfellows, as the old saying goes. With this we heartily concur. Ofttimes in the haste to make political friends, certain confusions occur, and the eagerly courted friends turn out to be a bit of a detriment—as in the following cases:

- The National Republican Congressional Committee (NRCC) bestowed a Republican-of-the-year award on one Mark A. Gretchen and sent him a letter informing him of the honor and inviting him to the awards luncheon. Gretchen, however, was unable to attend. He was serving a 26-year prison term for a sex offense. By way of explanation, an NRCC spokesman said simply, "We weren't aware of his current predicament." (We remain unsure as to whether Gretchen's award was rescinded.)

- "I write to invite you to join the President and Mrs. Bush for a private dinner here in Washington D.C. on June 19th and also to ask you to serve as a Special Representative of St. Clair, Ohio, at The President's Dinner. In fact, a special place of honor has already been reserved for you to recognize your steadfast support of President Bush."

  So said the invitation sent by Vice President Dick Cheney on May 8, 2002, to Robert Howard Kirkpatrick—who was serving 35 months at Ohio's Belmont Correctional Institution for drug possession. Cheney's office was most meticulous: The invitation was mailed to the lockup and included his inmate number in the address. We assume Kirkpatrick was unable to attend.

- "To win in 2000, I need you by my side."

  Al Gore, then campaigning, sent this direct-mail letter out, hoping to raise more support. Apparently, his campaign staffers were not that careful in screening the address list, though, as this particular letter was sent to someone who probably wouldn't have been swayed, no matter how eloquent the appeal: his opponent, George W. Bush.

- Senate Minority Leader Tom Daschle and Senator Jay Rockefeller decided to bring an "average" American to a press conference. He would be living, breathing proof of how beneficial the Clinton tax plan was. Rockefeller described the man as "a very close and personal friend." What he didn't say was that his "friend" had a small Nazi swastika near his right wrist.

- "Elizabeth and I are especially excited about the news of your nomination because we will have the chance to be with you."

  So said the letter signed by Bob and Elizabeth Dole and sent to rapper, self-confessed "woman beater," and drug dealer Eazy-E of the gangsta-rap group N.W.A. (Niggaz with Attitudes), informing him of his nomination to the Republican Senatorial Inner Circle.

Great Moments in Pork-Barrel Legislation

Pork is not just "the other white meat." It is also government spending run amok; spending that is not requested by Congress, not competitively awarded nor requested by the president; spending not serving the public at large but rather a local or special interest. It also exceeds the prior year's funding or the budget request made by the president.

It *is*, however, testament to the good ol' American "can-do" spirit—but in this case, the "can-do" comes from the taxpayer, and the reward goes to the politician who requests the pork and, by so doing, garners the support of his or her constituents.

This is not a cheap matter. In 2002, the two top pork producers in Congress were Senator Ted Stevens (R-Alaska), who managed to pull $451.3 million (which comes to $711 per Alaskan), and Senator Dan Inouye (D-Hawaii) with $432 million (or $353 per Hawaiian). This is not to say that other members of Congress have fallen down on the job. According to the watchdog group Citizens Against Government Waste, Congress spent a record $20.1 billion in 2001. Perhaps it is simple coincidence, but a lot of pork winds up going to the districts that happen to be served by those senators or congresspersons serving on their respective appropriations committees.

In perusing the following, you will note that pork knows no party. Republicans and Democrats alike seem to thrive on a high-fat diet when it comes to appropriating taxpayer money that just might win them votes.

Politician/State	Amount	For
Senator Ernest "Fritz" Hollings (D–South Carolina)	$14 million	to build the Hollings Marine Laboratory
Comments: Hollings got another million for the Hollings Cancer Center and was given the Narcissist Award by Citizens Against Government Waste, one of their annual Oinkers of the Year Awards		
Senator Richard Shelby (R–Alabama)	$2 million	to clean the Vulcan monument
Comments: This statue was built in 1903 to represent Alabama in the 1904 World's Fair; it stands in Birmingham to pay tribute to the area's steel industry		

Politician/State	Amount	For
Representative Jack Kingston (R–Georgia)	$450,000	to restore chimneys on Cumberland Island

Comments: Cumberland Island is a vacation spot in Kingston's district

Politician/State	Amount	For
Representative Sam Graves (R–Missouri)	$273,000	to combat "Goth" culture in Blue Springs, Missouri
Texas (politician N/A)	$125,000	for Sire Power to sell frozen bull semen

Comments: Said semen is used for artificial insemination

Politician/State	Amount	For
(state N/A)	$500,000	to support the Popcorn Board

Comments: The Popcorn Board is a trade association of popcorn makers that "educates" people about popcorn, in part through a website that has the "Encyclopedia Popcornica"

Politician/State	Amount	For
California (politician N/A)	$3 million	to pay for dancing-raisin ads sponsored by the California Raisin Board
Senator Ted Stevens (R–Alaska)	$2.25 million	to provide winter recreation alternatives in Fairbanks

Quick Fun Pork Fact: Each year, the Army spends $2 million to $4 million on the century-old civilian-marksmanship program. The Army had recommended cutting the program, but Congress apparently felt this was too important a matter (and the National Rifle Association too strong a lobbying group, one may think) and has continued to fund it. The marksmanship program subsidizes NRA shooting competitions. In addition, Congress plans to assist in setting up a Corporation for the Promotion of Rifle Practice—by giving away Army rifles, ammunition, computers, and cold, hard cash—for a total of $80 million.

Outrageously Stupid Government Overspending

It might appear that one of the requisites to being a government worker or elected official is to have a facility for handling money. Or, more precisely, for *spending* money. Living large—on taxpayers' dollars, of course—seems to come easy to many government types. Herewith, some examples of truly inspired uses of public funds:

Oregon state employees get luxury SUVs

Not even two weeks after it was announced that the State of Oregon was facing a $700 million cash crisis, managers at the Department of Administrative Services authorized the purchase of a fleet of seven luxury Ford Excursions, the largest sport-utility vehicle in the United States. These SUVs, which included premium compact-disc stereos, cost more than $208,000. Department managers defended the necessary luxury expenditure: "I think by and large we've done pretty well," said spokesperson Karmen Fore.

Wisconsin governor Scott McCallum uses airplane for 41-mile trip

McCallum, who consistently labels local officials carefree spenders, spent $2,800 to fly 41 miles by airplane, a very short jaunt from Madison to Beloit. The purpose of the trip was to present a ceremonial check to a local potato-chip factory. Tim Roby of McCallum's office initially promised to answer criticism of this example of government waste but later changed his mind. "Who's going to make a judgment of whether or not it's an efficient use of the plane?" he asked a local reporter. "You?"

Secretary of the Air Force flies to football game ... uh, meeting with ROTC officials

In 1990, Secretary of the Air Force Donald Rice and his wife were flown by Air Force jet and U.S. taxpayer–funded jet fuel to Notre Dame University from Washington, D.C., on the day of the Air Force–Notre Dame football game. When taxpayer-watch groups complained about the $5,700 cost, Rice's spokesperson explained that Rice had traveled there to discuss "official business" with ROTC candidates at the school.

U.S. ambassador to the U.N. gets $600,000 kitchen

John Negroponte, U.S. ambassador to the United Nations, was in a pickle during the debates about Iraq and the questions his government raised about the relevancy of the U.N. No, the matter at hand wasn't about Iraq, nor about the U.N.'s relevance. Rather, it was that the kitchen in his apartment at New York's luxury Waldorf-Astoria Hotel was a little too small (a mere 10 feet by 17 feet) to accommodate the needs of his guests. (Previous ambassadors seemed to have no problem with the kitchen, but perhaps Negroponte's guests have bigger appetites.) The State Department rushed to the rescue, agreeing to fund renovations to the kitchen to the tune of $600,000. Said one department official (who asked to remain nameless), "Yeah, it's a lot of money, but it's a lot of work, and it's worth it."

Nice new multithousand-dollar drapes hide breast

Attorney General John Ashcroft spent $8,000 for drapes in the Great Hall of the Department of Justice. The well-known purported reason: He couldn't stand being photographed in front of two statues—one of them the Spirit of Justice with a single breast exposed.

Privitization: For a Kinder, Gentler, Fairer America

In the spirit of their forebears, the pioneers who had to make do with little, modern American government officials are coming up with innovative methods of cost cutting, sometimes hiring outside companies to do things that the public sector once did, sometimes charging for previously free services, and sometimes seeking new methods of doing business. The thought: Everything will cost less, but the country will still run smoothly.

Granted, there is sometimes a downside to these methods. True bureaucrats don't pay attention to the negatives, though—especially if they have no direct impact on them. . . .

Some of these kinder, gentler, fairer ideas:

Drill for oil in state parks

Former Texas Parks and Wildlife Commission member and oilman Tony Sanchez claims it's not only right but a civic benefit to let his private company drill for oil and gas on

MY STRUGGLE

Until 1992, U.S. Army bookstores sold Adolf Hitler's *Mein Kampf.* Finally, after complaints from the German government, the Army withdrew the book. Up to that point, they had been selling around 1,000 copies per year.

state land: "There would be no greater joy than to see a beautiful park that our children can go to and learn about the oil and gas industry."

Dump toxic waste in third-world countries

Larry Summers, recently President George W. Bush's secretary of the treasury, advocated, while serving as the chief economist for the World Bank, toxic-waste dumping in third-world countries. "I've always thought that underpopulated countries in Africa are vastly underpolluted," he said. And complaints are much less likely, he added.

Give government lakeside property free to rich developers

By law, if the Army Corps of Engineers, which owns 456 lakes in 43 states, wants to sell any of them, it must make private developers pay fair market value for them. But what if the private developer is a buddy of a senator in the state where the lake is? Then *sublease* the lake to another quasi-government organization and let *them* give the lake for free to the rich private developer. This is what (seemed to have) happened in Oklahoma, where Ronald Howell, the former finance chairman for Republican senator James Inhofe, received a free 50-year lease on land estimated by *The New*

York Times to be worth hundreds of thousands of dollars. The corps was unrepentant: "We're not in the business of telling states how to operate," said George Taub, head of the Corps's Natural Resources Division. "If they decide that . . . then that's none of our business." In fact, according to Howell, the Corps actually suggested the sublease. And others suggested that maybe, just maybe, if the developer hadn't been a buddy of the senator. . . .

Pay private loggers to cut down trees in national forests

The pristine Tongass National Forest, one of the last old-growth forests left in the United States, filled with 400-year-old giant Douglas firs and cedars, has been opened to private logging firms for timber harvesting. This privatization effort is lauded by the second Bush administration as a way to reduce the federal deficit. There's one minor hitch: Because the government charges a very low price per huge tree and agrees to build access roads for the loggers, the taxpayer is not only *not* making a profit but is actually *paying* to have the national forest logged. The fact that the logging companies made large contributions to the Bush election campaign is of course coincidental.

Great Moments in Armored Appliances

A quick look at two sadly underdiscussed breakthroughs made by the U.S. armed forces.

Yes, we are speaking of armored appliances.

PRIVATE-ENTERPRISE CORPSE REMOVAL

Why should public employees transport dead bodies? The Chicago police for years had complained that they've had to take dead bodies to the morgue. Officers hated the job: "Each time they move a body, they scrub down the vehicle, which takes time," said a police spokesman. Finally, in March 2003, the city decided to open bids for anyone interested in carrying approximately 7,000 bodies per year; they must have six vans ready at all times. If interested, contact the Chicago city administration.

1. Crash-proof coffee machine

In the 1980s, the U.S. Air Force paid $7,000 for the installation of a coffeemaker in a passenger jet; the reason the price was so high was that the machine was guaranteed to survive a crash powerful enough to obliterate the entire crew.

2. Atomic-bomb-proof U.S. Air Force fax machines

In event of global thermonuclear war, the Air Force has fax machines that can survive—173 of them, each costing $547,000, all from Litton Industries. An investigation by Senator Carl Levin (D-Michigan) found that Magnavox had offered bomb-proof faxes for only $15,000 a unit, but the Air Force rejected the proposal: The Magnavox ones transmit only "newspaper"-quality images; the Litton Industries ones transmit "magazine"-quality images.

Why the U.S. Government
Should Not Sell Stuff on eBay

The idea behind selling things at an auction is simple: to make a profit. Usually, you try to make as large a profit as reasonably possible. In other words, why sell a car for $1,000 when you can sell it for $2,000? That's the way eBay works; that's the way most auctions work. You try to MAXIMIZE your profits. There are things you can do to make more money. You can: (1) set a decent opening price; (2) set a reserve price—a price below which you won't sell the item; (3) you can advertise and try to get as many bidders as possible.

Sound simple?

It is, but not for the brain-challenged employees of the U.S. Energy Department. They held an auction—and violated every rule of auctioning in the book. Here's what an official audit found about U.S. Department of Energy auctions. They had the biggest bargains in the century.

Item listed	Value	Price sold at
Twenty-three trucks	$448,000	$0.17 (yes, seventeen cents)
Copier	$9,000	$0.05 (one copy costs more than the copier)
Intel supercomputer (one of the 100 fastest computers in the world)	$89,000	$31,000 (after it was sold, the department bought it back . . . for $89,000)
Drilling rig	$3.9 million	$248,000

Those Wacky VA Administrators

A search of Department of Veterans Affairs office computers found evidence that roughly one third of files were devoted to things that were "obviously not for official use." Besides genealogy programs and computer games were photos of "models in swimwear." A VA spokesperson said, "There were just women in bathing suits. Nothing nude or in compromising positions."

Day Care at the CIA

According to a *Chicago Tribune* report, day care at the CIA is a little different: "The tots are identified by a first name and a number, such as Johnny 10.... [D]ay-care attendants, diaper changers, and the like have to undergo polygraph tests and an FBI check. The children of parents who are in CIA 'covert' work are sometimes kept separate from the kids of parents in 'overt' work."

Political Spelling

You may not have known this, but apparently an ability to spell is not a requirement should one choose to run for office. For example: When candidates for office in Charleston, West Virginia, handed in their official filing forms to the city clerk's office, four Democrats spelled their party name as "Democart" or "Democrate," while two Republicans spelled their party name as "Repbulican" and "Repucican." "I was kind of rushed," said Al Carey, a Republican challenger in the

Eighth Ward, who spelled his party "Republulican." And on the Democrat side? "I was rushed," explained Dana Griffith.

The Top Ten Stupidest Examples of Bureaucratic Blather

10. If the United States is attacked, file this page in book III of FPM Supplement 990-1, in front of part 771. Effective upon an attack on the United States and until further notice: a. Part 771 is suspended.

    —from the Federal Personnel Manual, Manual Supplement 990-3, Civil Service Commission, Part M-771, Employee Grievances and Appeals

9. "Complex litigation," as used in these rules, includes one or more related cases which present unusual problems and which require extraordinary treatment, including but not limited to the cases ordinarily designated as "protracted" or "big."

    —from the local rules of the U.S. District Court in Seattle, Washington

8. The increase in male unemployment for men between 1966 and 1972 can be fully explained by the almost continuous fall in male employment in this period.

    —Department of Employment's Employment Gazette

7. Exit access is that part of a means of egress that leads to an entrance to an exit.

    —government fire-prevention pamphlet for homes for the elderly

6. After a thorough investigation, we are able to determine that the late arrival of your mail was due to a delay in transit.

   —postal-service reply to a complaint

5. Because of the Veterans Day holiday next Wednesday, this release will be published on Friday, November 13th, instead of on Thursday, November 12th. It will be issued on Thursday, November 19th, its usual publication date, but will be delayed the following week until Friday, November 27th, because of the Thanksgiving holiday on Thursday, November 26th.

   —Federal Reserve memo, 1992

4. In such jurisdictions, the low HOME rent will have increased and, in some cases, will exceed the high HOME rent. In cases where the low HOME rent exceeds the high HOME rent, the rent applicable to a unit subject to the low HOME rent may not exceed the lower of the rents under 92.252(a)(1), i.e., the applicable high HOME rent.

   —from a memo by Gordon McKay, director of the Office of Affordable Housing, U.S. Department of Housing and Urban Development

3. In other words, feediness is the shared information between toputness where toputness is at a time just prior to the inputness.

   —U.S. Department of Education

2. Due to an administrative error, the original of the attached letter was forwarded to you. A new original

has been accomplished and forwarded to AAC/JA (Alaskan Air Command, Judge Advocate office). Please place this carbon copy in your files and destroy the original.

—a memo from the Alaska Air Command

1. This document did not concern you. Please erase your initials and initial your erasure.

—U.S. Army personnel department, Fort Baker

Well-Meaning Stupidity: When Good Intentions Go Bad

"The best laid plans of mice and men gang aft agley."

So wrote poet Robert Burns who, being Scots rather than American, phrased it differently than we might. Apparently, Burns was trying to say that good plans sometimes blow up in one's face. They simply don't work. They gang badly . . . and aft, at that.

Yes, all too often, in spite of planning and intent, plans most definitely go agley, as one might but probably doesn't often say, as "agley" is rarely used. ("Gang," however, is more widely used, particularly in East L.A. and New York City, most often accompanied by the words "Bloods" or "Crips.")

Following are rules that anyone planning a heartwarm-

Members of the Czech Heritage Society were finally asked to leave the Texas State Capitol in Austin, Texas, after serenading legislators, their staff, and local lobbyists for over three hours in German and Czech.

ing, quintessentially American lovefest and/or tribute should adhere to, to avoid having a moving ceremony descend down the slippery slope of stupidity. Ignore said rules at your own peril and potential loss of dignity.

Rule #1: If the tribute involves birds, get the right kind of birds—and get them early

Organizers for a 9/11 anniversary tribute in Jersey City discovered this a little too late. They had planned to release a flock of doves at the ceremony but they waited too long to order the doves; doves were sold out. They substituted pigeons for doves. Unfortunately, these pigeons had been in cages most of their lives, so when released they flew wildly into the assembled crowd, smashed into office building windows, and plummeted into the Hudson River.

Rule #2: Double-check everything before unveiling commemorative plaques

Lauderhill, Florida, held a ceremony in tribute to Martin Luther King's life at which a plaque honoring actor and activist James Earl Jones was unveiled. It read: *Thank you James Earl Ray for keeping the dream alive.* Unfortunately, James Earl Ray was Martin Luther King's assassin.

Rule #3: If honoring an individual, be sure you have the right name

The Chicago City Council voted to establish December 4 as Fred Hampton Day. Hampton was a Black Panther leader who was shot to death when police raided his apartment. After the vote, 16 white members of the council objected. They said that they thought they were honoring Chicago Bears defensive linebacker *Dan* Hampton.

Stupid Reactions to Terrorism in the U.S.A.

On the face of things, terrorism is surely not a humorous topic. With this we concur. But there have been some stupid things done as a result of terrorism which prove the unquenchable American spirit . . . and the consequent ability to turn something serious into something somewhat . . . silly.

Stupid Airline Passengers

After 9/11, airport security tightened. One might assume (with logic) that fewer passengers would attempt to bring certain items on board a plane.

This would be an incorrect assumption.

- During the 2001 Thanksgiving holiday, immediately after increased security was imposed at airports due to the 9/11 attacks, the following were confiscated from passengers:

  15,982 pocketknives

> 98 box cutters
>
> 6 guns
>
> 1 brick ("I don't know why he was carrying a brick," said a spokesman for the Transportation Security Administration.)

- At the 38 busiest U.S. airports:

  > 1,072 clubs or bats
  >
  > 3,242 banned tools
  >
  > 2,384 flammable items (including a welding gun in Boise, Idaho)
  >
  > 20,581 sharp objects (such as scissors, ice picks, and meat cleavers)
  >
  > 1 toy cannon made of live ammunition

- An American Airlines flight made an unscheduled landing in Salt Lake City to eject a college-student passenger after he tried to recharge an AA battery by heating it with a cigarette lighter.

- A passenger was detained at Lambert Field in St. Louis when his checked luggage was found to have a suspicious item: an alarm clock that had six toy sticks of dynamite attached to it.

- A Medford, Oregon, man was running a little late for his flight, so he came up with a not-so-brilliant way to ensure his flight was delayed long enough for him to get onboard: He called in a bomb threat. After phoning America West headquarters with his faux threat, he wandered over to the America West desk at the airport, asking about the flight . . . which was on its way back to the gate. The clerks got suspicious and called the police—so the man missed his flight after all *and* was held on outstanding unrelated criminal charges, not to mention for questioning by the FBI.

In a "credit where credit is due" spirit, let us also make note of those overzealous airport security screeners—who certainly are doing their darndest, gol'durnit, to keep us safe from a wide range of possible threats, including:

Suspicious Item: airline captain's personal pocketknife

An airline captain had his pocketknife, which had a one-inch blade, confiscated at New York's La Guardia Airport before he boarded the Boeing 757 he was going to fly to Florida. Reason: He was told that, if he kept the knife, he might use it to gain control of an airplane.

Suspicious Item: vibrators (of the sexually stimulating sort)

In February 2002, while in a plane on the runway in Dallas, 36-year-old Renee Koutsouradis was paged over the loudspeaker, asked to deplane and accompany a Delta Airlines security guard to the tarmac. There was "something suspicious" in her bag, something that appeared to be vibrating. She told the guard what she thought it was but was still asked to remove the item and hold it up for inspection. The item: a battery-operated sex toy she and her husband had bought while vacationing in Las Vegas—which she had apparently not switched off. According to the lawsuit she later filed against Delta, passengers on the plane saw her holding the item and began laughing at her; the three male Delta employees "began laughing hysterically" and made "obnoxious and sexually harassing comments." She is seek-

In an attempt to avoid promulgating the mistaken impression that only those who travel by air stoop to stupid levels, we present the following:

Six passengers were ejected from a Carnival Cruise Lines ship for bringing aboard 16 live, bottled bees—an "alternative" medication for one of the six, who has multiple sclerosis.

ing unspecified damages on a number of counts, including intentional infliction of public humiliation.

Suspicious Item: teeny-tiny G.I. Joe plastic toy guns

Eager to stick to the letter of the law, airport security screeners have, regardless of size, seized toy guns, even though the guns in question are unlikely to be used in a hijack attempt. Two recent cases: Screeners at Los Angeles International Airport discovered a G.I. Joe doll in a British tourist's carry-on luggage and confiscated it . . . because the doll carried a two-inch rifle. Explained an LAX spokesman: "We have instructions to confiscate anything that looks like a weapon or a replica. If G.I. Joe was carrying a replica then it had to be taken from him." (Alert officials also asked if the doll came equipped with replica hand grenades, which they also wanted to confiscate.) Similarly, the screeners at the Central Wisconsin Airport in Mosinee, Wisconsin, confiscated a G.I. Joe and the larger *four*-inch rifle it carried.

Suspicious Item: breast milk

Security guards at JFK International Airport in New York were suspicious about three bottles of milk that a woman was carrying (along with her infant daughter). The woman explained that it was breast milk for her daughter and offered to put a bit on her arm and lick it off to prove it wasn't a dangerous substance. But the guards said she had to drink from all three bottles or she would not be allowed on the plane. As the woman explained, they said that "there could be explosives in the baby bottles, and I could throw something at the stewardesses." She was considering a lawsuit, saying, "It was very uncomfortable and very embarrassing and very disgusting."

Suspicious Item: spray cologne

A Saudi Arabian college student was stopped at a security checkpoint at Philadelphia International Airport. His visa was fine, but security was worried about a container of liquid in his luggage. The student sprayed himself with the liquid, trying to show that it was merely cologne . . . but accidently also sprayed two security guards. A code-red hazardous-materials alert was issued, and local police, firefighters, and the FBI rushed to the scene. The guards were sent to a hospital for testing, and the emergency room was quarantined for three hours. A doughnut shop and a Rite Aid drugstore were also closed for forty-five minutes, after it was learned that two police officers had been to both after having come into contact with the "substance" when examining the bottle. The quarantines and the alert were lifted when the "unknown substance" was determined to be, indeed, cologne.

Suspicious Item: refillable lighters (but not disposable lighters)

On Christmas Day in the San Francisco Airport, a man was stopped at the security station. He had two cigarette lighters: a disposable Bic lighter and a refillable butane lighter that had been a gift from his wife. The security supervisor explained to him that the refillable lighter was not

THE ULTIMATE NO-BOMB SOLUTION

Kudos to Sacramento International Airport, which has put up a sign showing a cartoon of a bomb with a fuse sticking out of it and the International NO symbol over it (red slash). The assumption is that this will inform all passengers that one cannot bring a bomb on board a plane.

We feel very safe now.

permitted. The Bic, however, was fine. After being told he had two choices—mailing the lighter to himself or having it confiscated, the man went outside and kept lighting the lighter until it was out of butane. He went back in line and again was told he couldn't bring the lighter, even empty, on the plane. He could, however, still bring the disposable lighter. After arguing, he gave up and let them confiscate the empty lighter. The following day, he reached the chief of security, who explained that the lighter shouldn't have been confiscated and said he would try to get it back for him. The man described the lighter: brushed aluminum with a Mirage Casino logo. A few days later, he received a package in the mail containing a refillable butane lighter with a Mirage Casino logo . . . but it was black and gold.

Suspicious Item: mousetraps

Tampa airport screeners spotted a "very, very suspicious" object on their baggage-screening monitors and had a section of the airport evacuated for about forty-five minutes. A bomb squad was called in to remove the object from the suitcase. It was a mousetrap inside a coffee can.

U.S. Marines headed for Iraq were boarding a chartered commercial airliner when they were stopped by security. They weren't allowed to board while carrying their knives. No problem . . . they relinquished their knives and boarded the plane—carrying their M16 rifles and M60 machine guns.

Top Seven Stupid Terror-Related Overreactions

Here we honor those who—faced with the new U.S.A. in which the threat of terrorism was a new, distinct possibility—took matters to an amazing extreme.

Possibly Terroristic Oscar Mayer Wienermobile

A 27-foot-long hot-dog vehicle—the venerable Oscar Mayer Wienermobile—caused an alert on a Washington, D.C., road. The Wienermobile driver had gotten lost and inadvertently wound up on a road near the Pentagon that had been closed to commercial traffic since 9/11. Security officers, who man the road 24/7, pulled the motorized hot dog over to investigate . . . and found no problems. Said Virginia State Police spokeswoman Lucy Caldwell: "Obviously, this was a mistake. This hot dog posed no threat to us."

Hazardous Mail

It was a stained white envelope, and it was addressed to a congressperson, Representative Dana Rohrbacher (R-California). It definately looked suspicious. A postal worker who handled it complained of a headache and a "burning sensation"—he checked in at Unity Hospital, where concerned officials called in the FBI. The FBI promptly activated its Joint Terrorism Task Force, and two agents descended into the post office basement, where they gently and carefully opened the suspicious envelope and found . . . a potato slice. Maybe they should have read the envelope. It said "Have a French Fry," presumably a sarcastic reference to the House renaming the fries served in its cafeteria "freedom fries" in March 2003. No one was charged for terroristic threats, and the case was closed. Police explained that it is not threatening to suggest someone have a French fry, and it is not illegal to mail rotten potatoes.

Telemarketing Terrorist Fear

An official dispatch of the Branch County sheriff's department in Coldwater, Michigan, recently warned:

> [S]ome . . . telemarketing programs are believed to be operated by Al-Qaeda. The CIA has announced that they acquired a videotape showing Al-Qaeda members making phone solicitations for vacation home rentals, long distance telephone service, magazine subscriptions and other products.

A terrifying image: being sold a vacation time share in Orlando by Osama's thugs. There was one problem: All of this was information came from the September 18, 2002, edition of the satirical weekly *The Onion*. The detective who wrote the release was unaware that *The Onion* was a humor magazine but then said he got it all from the attorney general's office which had a link with *The Onion*, opening another can of worms. . . .

Building Evacuated over a Bottle

A package was found in an Orange County, California, building, leaking an unidentified fluid. Four workers immediately fell ill breathing the fumes. The building was immediately evacuated, and the Orange County Fire Department Hazardous Waste Team was quickly dispatched. Meanwhile, the ill workers were sent to local hospitals for treatment. The hazmat team carefully opened the package and found . . . a bottle of vodka. A fire department spokesman reassured worried people that the liquid was not toxic: "It's really only dangerous if they drink it and try to drive," he said.

Broadband Terror

Is broadband connected to terrorism? Jack Valenti, the perennial lobbyist for the film industry, seems to think so. In his own words, "There are more than nine and a half million broadband subscribers now. Once the pipes and high-speed access subscribers begin to increase, we can be terrorized by what is going on." Watch out, America.

Two 8-year-olds Face "Terrorist Threat" Charges

Two eight-year-olds at school in Irvington, New Jersey, were charged with making "terrorist threats" by "playing cops and robbers with a paper gun." Alert and vigilant local officials had caught the boys and filed charges.

Navy Opens Package Containing Overdue Library Book with Water Cannon

Terror fears are not new. Back in 1989, after a Navy electronics engineer was fired for blowing the whistle on wasteful practices at a base, he sent a return-receipt package of a base library book back to his commander, Captain Stephen Howard, along with his own return address. Howard, perhaps feeling guilty for firing the honest engineer, got the package and called in the bomb squad, which X-rayed it several times and declared that it was probably safe. Probably. The Navy took no chances. They fired a high-powered water cannon at the package and finally found that they had blown apart a book: *Engineering Contracts and Specifications*. The honest whistleblower was surprised. "If I had wanted to send a bomb," he asked, "why in the world would I send it return-receipt requested?" The Navy had no comment.

Hazmat Team Called over Potentially Hazardous Dead Mariners Fan

A Mariners fan's last wish was to have his ashes scattered over Safeco field. True to his wish, charter-plane company Wings Aloft was hired, and the container with the fan's ashes was flown over the stadium roof. . . . Unfortunately, several problems arose. First of all, it was 2002, and terror threats were in the air, and soon so was the container of ashes, which suddenly broke loose from the plane. Instead of ashes gently wafting through the air, the container hurtled down through the stadium's roof and burst into a cloud of dust inside. Terrified stadium workers below called for reinforcements—and an emergency hazmat team was mobilized and rushed to the field.

Man Decides to Test Pentagon Terrorism Alertness

Worried that the Pentagon might not be telling the truth when it said its antiterrorism system worked, a 43-year-old

⭐ STRETCHING THINGS

American businesses didn't take 9/11 lying down. Rather, some saw it as the perfect scapegoat for any possible financial problems. Among the companies and business leaders who claimed that 9/11 had a deleterious effect on their business:

Jack Daniel's whiskey

PalmPilot

Planet Hollywood

Martha Stewart

Donald Trump

Lenox china

Steve Madden shoes

Scottish pubs

Florida man decided to put it to the test. He sent an e-mail falsely threatening a "widespread attack on Patrick Air Force Base and the surrounding area." He should have been happy to know that the system *did* work, as he was traced and arrested. The man, with no prior criminal history, now faces up to 15 years in prison and a $10,000 fine if convicted.

What <u>Not</u> to Do During Terror Alerts

As a public service to any art students or conceptual artists, we tell you this cautionary tale, in the event you feel compelled to see the art possibilities in an Orange alert.

Restrain your artistic sensibilities! Which is what a School of Visual Arts student *didn't* do.

GREAT MOMENTS IN FBI SURVEILLANCE

At first, the FBI denied it. Then it admitted it. It WAS flying a spy plane over Bloomington, Indiana. The (bizarre) reason: It was watching for places where foreigners might be faxing or e-mailing late at night.

On December 11, 2001, three months to the day after the 9/11 attacks—37 boxes were discovered throughout the busy NYC Union Square subway station. Some of the boxes were painted black, others were wrapped in tape; all had the word "FEAR" painted on them. The station was evacuated for six hours, and the bomb squad was called in.

It turned out to be part of a sculpture-class project. Clinton Boisvert, 25, was simply commenting on the fear that permeated New York City. Cops were not amused by the "comment" and arrested him on charges of reckless endangerment and disorderly conduct. His teacher didn't say what his grade would be on this particular project but noted that he was an A student.

Stupid Hypocrisy, Prejudice, and Lame Excuses (and Political Correctness, Too) in the U.S.A.

Hypocrisy, prejudice, lame excuses, and political correctness are not uniquely American by any means. But, with typical American zest and zeal, Americans seem to have a special knack for doing them exceptionally well. . . .

Do as I Say, Not as I Do:
Great Moments in American Hypocrisy

It seems it is easy to take the moral high ground. However, adhering to one's own ethics appears to be not quite as easy, to judge by the following (somewhat stupid) examples.

Palmetto, Florida, community-redevelopment agency

What they're supposed to say: Let's help poor people find living space.

What they actually did: Evicted 40 Hispanic migrant workers—a week after Christmas—to make way for Habitat for Humanity, which intended to build low-income housing on the site.

The Lower East Side Tenement Museum, New York City

What they're supposed to say: Let's honor the struggles and lives of New York's immigrant and blue-collar tenement dwellers.

What they actually did: Tried to use eminent domain to seize the building next door and evict its blue-collar worker and immigrant tenants.

Teamsters Local 988, Houston, Texas

What they're supposed to say: Let's always go union.

What they actually did: Built a new union meeting hall using nonunion labor . . . since, as Local 988 officials said, "Union contractors cost too much."

Anti-SUV activists Gwyneth Paltrow and Chevy Chase

What they're supposed to say (and did): Let's not use gas-guzzling, unsafe SUVs. Paltrow appeared in ads for TV producer Norman Lear's Environmental Media Association (EMA), which accused SUV owners of supporting terrorism, and Chase has spoken in support of EMA.

What they actually did: Paltrow drives a Mercedes-Benz

SUV . . . which she, according to neighbors quoted in a *New York Post* story, parks on the sidewalk. Chevy Chase and his wife drive in their Westchester town in an SUV, but, says his rep, "They hate having the SUV and they're going to get rid of it as soon as the carmakers come out with a hybrid version."

Former CBS morning-show host Bryant Gumbel

What he's supposed to say: As journalists, let's strive for objectivity and unbiased coverage.

What he actually did: After an interview with conservative pundit Robert Knight on *The Early Show*, Gumbel was caught on camera mouthing the words, "What a fucking idiot."

Matthew J. Glavin, leader of a conservative legal foundation that sought to have Bill Clinton disbarred for his perjury and sexual peccadilloes

What he's supposed to say: Let's always keep it clean and honest.

What he actually did: Glavin was charged with public indecency after being caught fondling himself by a National Park Service Ranger. He also tried to fondle the ranger.

Representative Bob Barr (D-Georgia)

What he's supposed to say: Let's keep a cap on damage awards. He praised a bill before the House Judiciary, Commercial, and Administrative Law Subcommittee, which he chairs, that would cap damage awards for "pain and suffering" at $250,000.

What he actually did: The same day he praised that bill, he filed a lawsuit against President Bill Clinton, pundit

James Carville, and porn magnate Larry Flynt for $30 million, claiming "loss of reputation and emotional distress."

Chatham County state court DUI coordinator Brian P. Harell

What he's supposed to say: As the DUI coordinator, I always say, Don't drink and drive! (He had been working for two weeks as a coordinator of the Chatham County State Court DUI program—a pilot project aimed at helping DUI offenders avoid jail time by going on probation instead.)

What he actually did: He was arrested for drunk driving, with a blood alcohol level of .13 (the legal limit in Georgia is .08), after being stopped while driving at about 1:30 A.M. with no headlights on.

Boston city councilman Felix Arroyo

What he's supposed to say: I'm on a hunger strike to protest U.S. policy in Iraq.

What he really did: Amended the meaning of "hunger strike" by first saying he would have only liquids, then later that he would have only liquids during daylight hours (and food any other time), then still later that he would carry on this hunger strike only on the second and fourth Fridays of every month. In February 2003, he changed the strike again, choosing to fast every Friday of the month.

Ellen Fein, coauthor of bestselling relationship guide The Rules

What she's supposed to say: Let's follow my book *The Rules* and keep our marriages going strong (presumably by following such helpful tips as keeping your hair long since men find it more attractive, as well as needing to be subservient to your husband).

What she really did: She filed for divorce just after her third book, *The Rules for Marriage: Time-Tested Secrets for Making Your Marriage Work* was going to print. Fein and her coauthor noted in the book that "a Rules marriage is forever." Except for Fein's.

A quick list of men who have advocated military service and fighting most strenuously, and their personal contribution to America's proud military forces.

Name	U.S. Military Service	Comments
Vice President Dick Cheney	None	several deferments (said he "had other priorities")
Speaker of the House Dennis Hastert	None	bad knees (but wrestled in high school and college—and coached football and wrestling)
House Majority Leader Tom DeLay	None	tried to volunteer but claimed that all the available spots were taken up by minorities
Deputy Secretary of Defense Paul Wolfowitz	None	studied under nuclear strategist Albert Wohlstetter at the University of Chicago
Pundit Bill O'Reilly	None	was in college and grad school (including a year at the University of London)

Name	U.S. Military Service	Comments
Pundit Rush Limbaugh	None	couldn't serve due to a health problem—probably an anal cyst (although he has denied this, Limbaugh biographer Paul D. Colford has confirmed this in print)

WHAT A DIFFERENCE THREE YEARS MAKE. . . .

Green Bay Packers tight end Mark Chmura refused to visit the White House in 1997 as part of the Super Bowl–winning Packers team, citing the immorality of Bill Clinton's affair with Monica Lewinsky. Three years later, he was charged with sexually assaulting a 17-year-old girl at a postprom party.

"It Wasn't My Fault"

Many Americans pride themselves on what used to be called "the gift of gab." Americans tend to be known all over the world for their glibness, their ability to schmooze, their readiness to talk. (This might explain the high pay of talk-show hosts and morning-news personalities. Then again, it might not.)

This gift is particularly beneficial when used to explain away a problem. But as the following demonstrate, all too often said silver tongue lacks the correct chemical structure. Consider these helpful suggestions of what *not* to say when caught in a sticky situation:

Allegation: sexually abusing a 13-year-old boy

Lame Excuse: "My hand slipped [onto a] private area."

—said by New York City choir official Frank Jones, who had been massaging the boy with cream when his hand . . . slipped.

Allegation: intent to sexually abuse a minor, having been discovered in a motel room with 60 bondage and sex toys, Viagra, and a child-porno photograph

Lame Excuse: Regarding the Viagra and sex toys—they were just props. As for the child-porn shot—"[It] helps motivate me" in working to hunt down and stop adults who sexually abuse children.

—said by professed vigilante against child sexual abuse Gordon Neal Diem, who was convicted after he attempted to arrange a meeting in his motel room with two teenage girls he'd met online. One of the "girls" was a police officer who interestingly didn't believe Diem's story.

Allegation: lying about academic, military, and work records, claiming (falsely) that you have a master's degree in psychology, served in Vietnam, and worked for the CIA

Lame Excuse: (1) My wife typed the application forms.

(2) I didn't believe certain biographical and educational information was important.

(3) I suffer from a little-known medical condition called *Pseudologia fantastica* and can't help telling lies and mixing fantasy and fact.

—claims made by Los Angeles judge Patrick Couwenberg after it was found that he had falsified his background and lied to the governor in a (failed) effort to get a juicy judicial appointment.

Allegation: intent to rob (but got caught in the chimney)
Lame Excuse: I was stargazing and slipped into the chimney.

> —excuse made by 19-year-old Josh Perez of San Diego, who was stuck in a chimney for five hours before rescuers could free him. He wound up being arrested on a burglary charge.

Allegation: nuclear-plant operators sleeping on the job
Lame Excuse: "It depends on your definition of asleep. They weren't stretched out. They had their eyes closed. They were seated at their desks with their heads in a nodding position."

> —explanation given by Commonwealth Edison Supervisor of News Information John Hogan, responding to a charge by a Nuclear Regulatory Commission inspector that two Dresden, Illinois, nuclear-plant operators were sleeping on the job.

Allegation: frequenting strip club
Lame Excuse: "First, it was not a strip bar, it was an erotic club. And, second, what can I say? I'm a night owl."

> —said by Marion Barry, mayor of Washington, D.C., after being found in a so-called gentlemen's club.

Allegation: sharks attacking beachgoers
Lame Excuse: "It wasn't a shark attack, but a shark *accident.* More than likely he ran into [the swimmer's] leg and got it caught in his mouth."

> —spin attempt made by Joe Rubio, South Padre Island, Texas, town spokesman hoping to quell rumors that a woman had been attacked by a shark while swimming at the beach.

Great Moments in Political Correctness, American-style

In an effort to counteract racism, sexism, homophobia, et al., many American institutions and individuals do the time-honored American thing: They bend over backward to be absolutely, positively sure that nothing is being done or said that could be, in the least way, construed as offensive.

This well-intended gymnastic move often results in situations that aren't as much inoffensive as ineffably ridiculous.

P.C. bombs

During the Afghan and Iraqi wars in 2001–2003, soldiers were told to watch out when writing the traditional messages on bombs before they were launched. Once, during the Iraqi war, someone wrote an anti-French message on a bomb; concerned senior officers said that it definitely "crossed the line." They went on the lookout for any other negative messages about the French. Sailors on the USS *Enterprise* were admonished by Rear Admiral Stephen Pietropaoli after one of them wrote a homophobic message on a bomb destined for the Taliban. His exhortation: "Keep the messages [on bombs] positive."

"Rogue states" sounds too judgmental

In the late 1990s, Secretary of State Madeleine Albright ordered the State Department to soften the term "rogue state," as applied to nations such as North Korea. The new official term for rogue states: "states of concern."

"Stunt fish" and plastic bottles used in fishing movie

A River Runs Through It was a poignant book about the joys of fishing. In making the movie, producers were careful not to act like fishermen and hurt real fish. In fishing scenes, actors' lines were tied to submerged plastic bottles—and for close-ups "stunt fish" were used . . . under Humane Society supervision, of course.

Group calls for an end to animal "pornography"

Feminists for Animal Rights (FAR), which attempts "to expose the connections between sexism and speciesism," called for a more sensitive media portrayal of animals in, among other things, cartoons. "The distorted images of animals displayed in the media, language, advertising, and cartoons distorts and degrades animals. Is this not another form of pornography?"

"Hate groups" sounds unfriendly

In the antibigotry resolution of Walworth County, Wisconsin, in 1995, a reference calling "white supremacists" members of "hate groups" was changed, since using the word "hate" was too judgmental. "Hate group" was changed to "unhappy group."

Children's books denigrated for sexism

According to an antibias-curriculum handbook, there are many dangerous kids' books out there. Babar the elephant extols "the virtues of a European middle class life-style and disparages the animals and people who have remained in the jungle," according to Patricia Ramsay of the Gorse Child Studies Center. Cinderella is particularly dangerous.

After Florida passed an "English-only" law barring counties from spending public funds to provide services in any language but English, the Dade County zoo changed its animal-name signs, omitting the Latin names of species.

According to Debra Goldsbury, "This story is not fun for me. Cinderella isn't making decisions for herself or taking charge of her own life."

State representative introduces bill requiring men to get written permission for sexual intercourse

In the 1990s, Oklahoma state representative Cleta Deatherage introduced a bill that would have required men to get written permission from any female with whom they intended to have sex; in addition, men would be required to warn females that sex could be hazardous and might result in pregnancy.

Prejudice: Can't We All NOT Get Along Awards

Let us pause here and celebrate the many facets of prejudice existing in the U.S.A. With typical democratic (with a small "d") zeal, Americans apply prejudice to a wonderfully wide range of people in our republican (with a small "r") country. One can be an equal-opportunity bigot here and choose one's target from a myriad of choices. But prejudice, as with anything, can become a tad . . . tired. Run-of-the-mill. Even boring.

We are happy to note that there are those, however, who bravely take prejudice to new, ever-rising heights. And we are proud, indeed humbled, by offering awards to these folks. Herewith, the first Can't We All *NOT* Get Along Award winners—the most fascinating and/or mind-boggling examples of American prejudice in action (cue the "God Bless America" soundtrack, please):

In the Racism Division

The I Wish I'd Never Heard *of Strom Thurmond Award goes to . . . Senator Trent Lott (R-Mississippi)* . . . who got caught with his foot in his mouth at a 100th birthday party for retiring senator Strom Thurmond. While praising Thurmond—who had run for the presidency in 1948 on an anti-integration platform—Lott talked about his state, Mississippi, one of the four states Thurmond carried, saying: "We're proud of it. And if the rest of the country had followed our lead, we wouldn't have had all these problems over all these years either." To make matters worse for him, reports of similar, earlier, comments of his hit the media, such as, "You know, if we had elected this man thirty years ago, we wouldn't be in the mess we are today," which Lott was quoted as saying of Thurmond in 1980. Lott tried to explain away his birthday-party comment, saying he had meant only to pay tribute to Thurmond's long political career during a "lighthearted affair."

The Let's Call a Spade a Spade Award goes to . . . the Branford, Connecticut, Rainbow Girls. When blacks were excluded from membership in this girls' club/service group, one of the leaders answered charges of racism very succinctly: "We haven't had any problem here about race. We just don't go for letting the colored ones in."

The Colorful Racist/Religious Intolerance Commentary Award goes to . . . New York Post *columnist Daniel Pipes . . .* who, in writing about accused D.C.-area sniper John Allen Muhammad, commented that he was not surprised he was an African American because "it fits into a well-established tradition of American blacks who convert to Islam turning against their country."

The That Could Well Be a Load of Sheet Award goes to . . . the principal of Yosemite High School, California, Bob LaBelle . . . who, after the school awarded a best costume prize at their annual Halloween party to three teenagers—two wearing KKK sheets, the third in blackface pretending to be a lynching victim—explained: "We had to make a quick decision."

The Better Late Than Never Award goes to . . . the Mississippi state legislature . . . which, in March 1994, finally approved a resolution ratifying the U.S. constitutional amendment banning slavery.

The There's Nothing Like a Stereotype Between Friends Award goes to . . . the U.S. division of Toyota and Jet *magazine . . .* which both were involved in a not-so-great moment in American advertising. In 1998, the U.S. division of Toyota ran an ad in *Jet* magazine (devoted to African-American readers) for a Toyota Corolla, which said, "Unlike your last boyfriend, it goes to work in the morning." Toyota and *Jet* shortly afterward issued an apology to readers.

The Can't You Take a Joke? Award goes to . . . federal judge Alan McDonald . . . who, during a court session in which a black man was testifying, wrote "Ah is im po tent." McDonald refused to apologize, saying the notes were not intended for the public and besides were being misrepresented.

The Spellcheck Needed Award goes to . . . MSNBC . . . which put up an on-screen caption during an interview with Republican consultant Niger Innis that identified him as "Nigger Innis." "It's not the first time it's happened," said Innis, "but hopefully it's the last."

In the Anti-Semitism Division

The He Ain't Jewish, He's My Brother Award goes to . . . the president of the Dallas chapter of the NAACP . . . who told a radio interviewer he was "concerned" about then–vice presidential candidate Joseph Lieberman since Lieberman is Jewish and "we need to be very suspicious of any kind of partnerships between the Jews at that kind of level because we know that their interest primarily has to do with, you know, money and these kind of things."

The Umbrella of Diversity Award goes to . . . Kennebunk, Maine, and its code-enforcement officer . . . who told restaurant owner Brian Bartley that he had to cover up the words "Hebrew National Beef Franks" on the umbrellas outside his restaurant. The officer claims it's a violation of a sign ordinance, but Bartley says that the officer had told him that the umbrellas "personally offended" him.

In the Anti-Asian Division

The High IQ Award goes to . . . the unknown vandal . . . who spray painted GO BACK TO JAPAN on the Korean Presbyterian church in Glendale, California.

In the Anti-Indo-Pak-Arab Division

The Kwick-E-Mart Award goes to . . . Representative Susan Myrick (R–North Carolina) . . . who announced that the terrorist threat is more widely spread than we may have thought: "Look at who runs all the convenience stores across the country," she pointed out.

Homophobia

From a few experts, some wonderfully stupid tips on how to solve what some obviously consider the "problem" of rampant homosexuality in the United States:

Tip #1: Check their handshakes

Electronic Data Systems, while under the leadership of CEO Ross Perot, had the following in their recruiting policy: "Do not hire anyone who has a weak handshake; a person who has a weak handshake is probably gay and might have AIDS; do not hire gay people."

Tip #2: Ban gay-oriented books that might fall into the hands of impressionable youth

The school board of Merrimack, New Hampshire, voted in 1995 to ban all books that portray gay characters positively.

Tip #3: Better yet, destroy all (and we do mean all) gay books

John Perkyns, a 48-year-old San Francisco man, felt the need to destroy homosexual-themed books at two libraries. In his zeal, he also allegedly vandalized books by authors Gay Talese and Peter Gay . . . as well as a book about the airplane that dropped the bomb on Hiroshima: the *Enola Gay*.

Tip #4: Beware of "coded" language

Yet another school board—this one in Meridian, Idaho—asked a student human-rights group to revise its constitution, eliminating words such as "tolerance" and "cultural diversity." The school board chairman clarified: "We asked them to clean up the language so that it isn't oriented toward homosexuality."

Tip #5: Come right out and explain that gay sex is just this close to incest

Senator Rick Santorum (R-Pennsylvania) decided to give a helpful hint to the Supreme Court in 2003 regarding homosexuality. Commenting on a court challenge to a Texas ban on gay sex at home, Santorum said, in full political hairsplitting mode: "I have no problem with homosexuality. I have a problem with homosexual acts, as I would with acts of other, what I would consider to be, acts outside of traditional heterosexual relationships." He went on to equate consensual gay sex with other acts; to wit: "If the Supreme Court says that you have a right to consensual sex within your home, then you have the right to bigamy. Then you have the right to polygamy, you have the right to incest.... [Y]ou have the right to anything."

Tip #6: And always make sure to deliver your message with humor

Congressman Dick Armey (R-Texas), ever-humorous former House majority leader, not only once referred to openly gay congressman Barney Frank (D-Massachusetts) as "Barney Fag" but also managed to milk the "joke" even

THE SPECIAL "I HATE ALMOST EVERYONE" AWARD . . .

. . . goes to pitcher John Rocker: "I'm not a very big fan of foreigners. You can walk . . . in Times Square and not hear anybody speaking English. Asians and Koreans and Vietnamese and Indians and Russians and Spanish people. . . . How the hell did they get into this country? . . . Imagine having to take the 7 train . . . next to some kid with purple hair next to some queer with AIDS . . . next to some 20-year-old mom with four kids. It's depressing."

further. Asked by humorist Dave Barry, "Are you the real Dick Armey?" Armey came back with the following classic: "Yes, I am Dick Armey. And if there is a dick army, Barney Frank would want to join up."

The Time-Honored Washington, D.C., Sport of Sexism

Let us here honor those elected officials serving our nation in Washington, D.C., who have taken sexism and raised it to unparalleled heights:

The Charm and Couth Award goes to . . . Representative Martin Hoke (R-Ohio) . . . who, when getting ready to comment on-air about President Clinton's State of the Union address, noticed a female TV producer walking by and said (unaware that his mike was turned on . . . among other things), "She has the *beeeg* breasts."

The Cutesy-Wutesy Award goes to . . . Representative Joe Barton (R-Texas) . . . who said the following after the president of the Association for Commuter Transportation, Dee Angell, took too much time testifying before his committee: "It's only because you're so cute that I'm letting you get away with this."

The I'll Bet You Want an MRS. Degree Award goes to . . . Senator Strom Thurmond (R-North Carolina) . . . who told a group of women's leaders who were testifying before a Senate hearing: "These are the prettiest witnesses we have had in a long time. I imagine you all are married. If not, you could be if you wanted to be."

The I Know What I Like Award goes to . . . numerous congressmen . . . who stipulated their hiring requirements as follows:

> "a white girl, prefer Floridian."—Representative James. A. Haley (D-Florida)

> "white Republican."—Representative Vernon Thompson (R-Wisconsin)

> "white—no pantsuits."—Representative James Delaney (D–New York)

> "attractive, smart, young, and no Catholics and water signs."—Representative Bob Eckhardt (D-Texas)

The Press Relations Award goes to . . . Virginia state senator Hunter B. Andrews . . . who cleverly asked a female reporter: "Are you hot to trot this week?"

The Boobheaded Extrication Attempt Award goes to . . . Representative Ernest Konnyu (R–California) . . . who said to a 26-year-old female aide at a press conference, "Why you

A SPECIAL NOD TO SEXISM IN THE ARMED FORCES

Aside from the widely publicized Tailhook and Air Force Academy scandals, let us make note of these earlier incidents.

- Francine Adams, a U.S. Navy petty officer, asked the Navy for assistance after suffering a concussion from a beating by her former boyfriend, who showed up at her quarters drunk and unannounced. The Navy's helpful response to her plea for help: "Avoid abusive relationships. . . . Any further deficiencies in your performance and/or conduct . . . may result in disciplinary action."

- Two male sailors threw a female sailor over the side of a torpedo boat, according to the *Chicago Tribune*. They were sentenced to 30 days at hard labor. The abuse took place just after the crew had attended a daylong session on sexual harassment.

- Rear Admiral Louis Wilmot, commanding officer at the Naval Training Center in Orlando, Florida, for female recruits, commented on 24 allegations of rape and sexual harassment at the center by saying "We can assure young women and their parents that they have nothing to fear."

got your boob covered up?" then later tried to explain his comment away by saying, "She wore her name tag . . . right over her boobs. . . . I didn't think it was right for her to have her name tag on in a—it should be up high. She's not exactly heavily stacked, OK? . . . So I told her . . . to move the darn name tag off her boobs."

Stupid Food in the U.S.A.

A little snack break and some food for thought . . .

Waiter, There's a Pubic Hair in My Soup!

The United States can be justly proud: We probably have the cleanest food in the world, along with a handful of other countries like Switzerland, which are a lot duller than we are. On the other hand, at times we find strange things in our unusually clean food. . . .

My typical school-cafeteria sandwich

A Massachusetts student bit into the sandwich she got at her school cafeteria—and spit out part of a human thumb. The thumb piece belonged to a cafeteria worker, who had sliced off the tip in the vegetable slicer. Complained one student: "Our lunch is our most valuable time, and now we have to eat fingers."

What's that on my pizza?

Two people bought a pizza and found, in addition to cheese and tomato sauce, a pubic hair. Or so they claim in their lawsuit for more than $100,000 for pain and distress. According to the store owner, "This did not happen," but the couple claims the hair may belong to an employee of the pizza outlet who had had previous conflicts with one of them. They're doing the scientific thing: They've asked for DNA testing of the hair; and they've frozen the pizza to preserve the evidence.

Bat cheeseburger, hold the mustard

A not amazingly acute Lexington, Tennessee, man in 2002 was handed a cheeseburger by a restaurant worker. He did not look particularly closely at the bun or the cheeseburger. Had he done so, he might have noticed that it had a bony brown wing sticking out. Instead, he took a bite. That's when he heard a loud crunch, and, looking, he realized he had taken a bite out of a bat that had been wedged between two slices of a hamburger bun. Regarding the person serving him, he said, "I thought it was strange that she got a smirk on her face when I started to bite into the sandwich."

Sandwich roll with enamel

An Alamance, North Carolina, man drove up to his local Hardee's and got a sandwich roll—bacon, egg, and cheese . . . and an old human tooth. Hardee's denies there was a tooth with the eggs, but the man claims a Hardee's cook was later fired after admitting that it was his tooth that fell into the sandwich. The man is suing the company.

Kellogg's Chocolate Rice Krispies with . . . bacon? No, what is that?

An Ottawa, Ontario, schoolgirl was about to eat that good old American snack, a Rice Krispies square, chocolate flavor, when she noticed something funny in the square. It looked like a piece of thick bacon, but it had a head. It was a slug, with a long, dried-out body and a head buried in the square. The girl said, "Everyone was as grossed out as I was." In what is an understatement, she added, "It's just really weird that there would be a slug in it." Kellogg's seemed to agree it was "really weird." A spokesperson said that Kellogg's has high health and manufacturing standards, implying quite correctly that slugs are not compatible with high manufacturing standards.

Hold the pickles—and the burger, for that matter

A sheriff's deputy in the Rochester area of New York State became violently ill after eating at a Burger King. He had asked for a burger without a pickle or special sauce. This "have it your way" request apparently so infuriated a tightly wound Burger King worker that he retaliated by putting a new kind of topping on the deputy's burger: oven cleaner. The same worker at other times admitted that he spat or peed on burgers and also enjoyed skating on frozen burgers. "I thought it'd be funny, and it was a cool thing to do at the time," he said to the police and the judge after he was caught.

My burger is wiggling, my burger is wiggling

Not to be outdone by Burger King, McDonald's was sued by a Detroit family in 2001 in another unusual burger incident. An 11-year-old boy was biting into his cheeseburger when, in the word of this boy's lawyer, "his sister . . . standing next to him . . . starts freaking out, because she sees these things crawling around his mouth and out of his mouth. She starts screaming." Those "things," the boy's lawyer asserts, were maggots, and the boy allegedly swallowed six of them at least, after which he proceeded to vomit. The boy's family is suing for $1 million; McDonald's has called the lawsuit "questionable" and adds that it has not seen any evidence to support the claim. The family says they have saved all the evidence they need: the remains of the maggot-ridden cheeseburger, as well as, of course, the vomit.

Taco with real hot sauce

Sergeant Scott Bahr of Beaver Dam, Wisconsin, ordered a to-go order from Taco Bell and got a mouthful that literally burned the insides of his mouth. The swollen-mouthed police officer later discovered that it wasn't hot sauce that had burned him: Two workers had laced his food with a white, powdery bleach used to clean sinks.

I'll skip the salad bar . . .

In late 2000 and early 2001, if you got food from a salad bar in New York City and noticed a funny taste, it may not have been your overactive imagination. There may have been odiferous human feces in your tuna salad or pungent urine along with salad dressing in your spinach salad. Finally, in the spring of 2001, after customers noticed a man acting oddly at a deli in Midtown Manhattan, the truth came out. A 34-year-old man had apparently been dumping human waste products (his own, presumably) at delis around town, specifically at delis in or near Penn Station, Grand Central Terminal, and around 42nd Street.

My chicken tastes kind of . . . damp . . .

A man was arrested and charged with urinating on packages of chicken in a Dillon market in Jackson County, Kansas, in January 2003. He was charged under a new food-supply contamination law. Hopefully for buyers of pack-aged chicken, it was a first offense.

There's something that looks sort of like a . . . penis in my fruit punch

In 2001, a man in Commercial City, Colorado, spotted an unidentified three-inch cylinder floating in his Ora Potency Fruit Punch—unfortunately only after having drunk two thirds of it. He brought the offending drink and object to the police. The county coroner announced that "it resembles just what they think it is, but we're having it checked to make sure." The pathologist who examined the object shortly af-terward announced that it was indeed a penis. "If you saw it you would have believed it," she said. Bottles were taken off the shelves, and a second bottle with a similar object was found. Finally, after tests, the object was determined not to be a penis after all. It was just a chunk of penis-shaped mold; not as bad as a penis, but still not too appetizing.

Pop-Tart Blowtorches

Pop that Kellogg's Pop-Tart in your toaster and stand back as giant flames shoot out and blowtorch your kitchen. This is not the "family friendly" sort of advertising Kellogg's is interested in, but it is, alas for Kellogg's, apparently true.

Under certain circumstances, a Pop-Tart in the toaster can spew out large flares of flame, igniting a kitchen or even a home. In 1995, Kellogg's agreed to pay $2,400 in damages to the insurance company of Thomas Nagle, who claimed that a fire damaged his kitchen after a Pop-Tart he was toasting in 1992 combusted. Worse yet, in 2000, Brenda J.

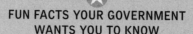

**FUN FACTS YOUR GOVERNMENT
WANTS YOU TO KNOW**

According to a finding in the U.S. Department of Agriculture's Marketing Research Report no. 1044, made after a detailed scientific study of cooks in 13 restaurants, it should take 34.5 seconds to prepare French toast for frying.

Hurff of Washington Township, New Jersey, put a cherry Pop-Tart in the toaster before taking her children to preschool. She came back to a burning home. She's suing for $100,000.

So what is it about Pop-Tarts? According to a wonderful website, www.pmichaud.com/toast/, where Patrick Michaud shows the results of his rigorous scientific experiment, if a Pop-Tart is trapped in a toaster, flames about 18 inches high can start erupting from the interaction of the heating coils of the toaster and those special Pop-Tart ingredients. Michaud says he used Kellogg's Strawberry Pop-Tarts with Real Smucker's Fruit; he suggests that a frosted variety of Pop-Tarts may result in higher or larger flames. P.S. Our lawyer asked us to tell you that YOU SHOULD NOT TRY THIS AT HOME! Mr. Michaud is a scientist conducting experiments under controlled conditions.

Food Records

We are proud to note that the U.S.A. holds an extremely large number of the world's records in a particularly grueling area: large food items.

This falls in line with the motto "Bigger is better." So say many Americans, who tend to apply this maxim to everything from penises to servings of fries. And so must say those involved in the following, who combine the good old American tradition of "trying to get into the *Guinness Book of World Records* for *anything*" with the "bigger is better" credo.

So herewith let us celebrate American ingenuity, pluck, and the urge to make extremely large food items, an area in which the U.S. clearly leads most of the rest of the world.

Food Item	Size	Ingredients	Where/When Made
World's Largest Rice Krispies Treat	12 ft. long, 6 ft. wide, 2 ft. deep; 2,480 lbs.	818 lbs. Rice Krispies, 1,466 lbs, marshmallows, 217 lbs. butter	Iowa State University, April 2001

Notes:

• Broke previous Rice Krispies Treat record (2,260 lbs.) set at Michigan State University

• Made in observance of the 2001 all-university theme "Strengthening Families to Become the Best"

• Honors alumna Mildred Day (a 1928 home-ec graduate), who helped create the prototype for the Rice Krispies Treat at Kellogg's

World's Largest Grilled Cheese Sandwich	5.5 ft. x 10.5 ft.; 320 lbs.	120 lbs. sharp cheddar cheese	Everglades City, Florida, during Second Annual Cheese and (Florida) Cracker Festival, November 4, 2000

Food Item	Size	Ingredients	Where/When Made

Notes:

- Made by Cabot Cheese
- A 1999 attempt at a world record was denied by Guinness, which had inadvertently sent the wrong guidelines. The Cabot/Everglades City team regrouped and tried again, this time successfully

Food Item	Size	Ingredients	Where/When Made
World's Largest Ham Biscuit	10.5 ft. in diameter; 400 lbs.	150 lbs. flour, 2 lbs. salt, 6.5 lbs. sugar, 39 lbs. shortening, 39 cups water, 13 gals. buttermilk, 16 large baked country hams	Cadiz, Kentucky, during Ninth Annual Ham Festival, 1985

Notes:

- A hotly contested large-food-item record (see below)

Food Item	Size	Ingredients	Where/When Made
World's *Second* Largest Ham Biscuit	8.5–9 ft. in diameter	500 lbs. Smithfield ham	Smithfield, Virginia, during 250th birthday celebration

Notes:

- Replica to be placed in proposed Ham Museum
- Unfortunately, didn't realize Cadiz had already made a larger ham biscuit; said one community volunteer, "When I contacted Guinness, there was no such thing as a ham category."

Food Item	Size	Ingredients	Where/When Made
World's Largest Enchilada	assembled from 10-ft.-wide tortillas	750 lbs. corn, 175 gals. vegetable oil, 75 gals. red chili sauce,	Las Cruces, New Mexico, during Las Cruces Whole Enchilada

Food Item	Size	Ingredients	Where/When Made
		175 lbs. grated cheese, 50 lbs. chopped onions	Festival, 2000

Notes:
- Took four hours to complete entire enchilada

Food Item	Size	Ingredients	Where/When Made
World's Largest Taco	16 ft. 2.5 in. x 31.5 in.; 1,144 lbs.	large flour tortilla, 943 lbs. fajita meat, 73.5 lbs. tomatoes, 47 lbs. chopped cilantro, 81 lbs. chopped onions	Houston, Texas, during Third Annual Taco Festival, May 4, 2000

Notes:
- Flour tortilla made by La Ranchera; filling by Mama Ninfa's Original Mexican Restaurant

Food Item	Size	Ingredients	Where/When Made
World's Largest Margarita / World's Largest Cocktail	mixed in 7,500-gal. FDA-approved polyethylene tank/margarita glass; 64,000 lbs. (glass and drink)	5,250 gals. margarita mix, 1,313 gals. tequila, 437 gals. triple sec	Key West, Florida, at Jimmy Buffett's Margaritaville restaurant

Notes:
- Equivalent of 44,800 20-oz. margaritas
- Took 2 days to make

Food Item	Size	Ingredients	Where/When Made
World's Largest Strawberry Shortcake	827 sq. ft.; 6,000 lbs.	NA	Plant City, Florida (the Winter Strawberry Capital of the World), February 19, 1999

Food Item	Size	Ingredients	Where/When Made
World's Largest Bagel	13.75 in. high; 59 in. in diameter; 714 lbs.	NA	Thirteenth Annual Bagel-fest Summer Festival, July 1998
World's Largest Doughnut	16 ft. in diameter; 3,739 lbs.	NA	Utica, New York

Notes:

• Combined effort of Hemstrought's Bakeries and radio station WKLL

Food Item	Size	Ingredients	Where/When Made
World's Largest Caesar Salad	4,395 lbs.	NA	San Francisco, California, 1998

Notes:

• Made to "celebrate the conservation of culinary arts in the city" by 25 volunteers from Moose's Restaurant and Assemblywoman Carole Migden

Food Item	Size	Ingredients	Where/When Made
World's Largest Garden Salad	7,248 lbs.	NA	Yuma, Arizona, during Yuma Lettuce Days

Notes:

• Made by 75 volunteers in 5 hours

• Previously had been no Guinness record for a salad made out of iceberg lettuce, the type grown predominantly in the Yuma area, but the record for salads made out of other lettuce was about 6,000 lbs.

Food Item	Size	Ingredients	Where/When Made
World's Largest Shrimp Cocktail (possibly)	2,000 lbs.	2,000 lbs. shrimp, plus lemon wedges and cocktail sauce	Las Vegas, Nevada, May 2002

Food Item	Size	Ingredients	Where/When Made

Notes:

- Made to celebrate opening of Seafood for Less
- Might actually be second place in Largest Shrimp Cocktail history, as a Mexican tourism website claims that Veracruz, Mexico, holds the title at 4,000 lbs. Guinness, however, was present at the Nevada construction

| World's (Second) Largest Pizza | 10,000 sq. ft.; 140 ft. across; 22 tons | 18,174 lbs. flour, 6,445 lbs. sauce, 9,375 lbs. cheese, 2,387 lbs. pepperoni | Havana, Florida, 1987 |

Notes:

- Was cut into 94,248 slices and eaten by more than 30,000 people

| World's Largest Cheesesteak | 365 ft. x 7 in.; 1,790 lbs. | NA | Philadelphia, Pennsylvania, 1998 |

Notes:

- Made in parking lot before an Eagles-Giants football game to help boost attendance during dismal season. The Eagles lost the game

| World's Largest Potato Chip | 23 x 14.5 in. | NA | Jackson, Tennessee, but on exhibit at Idaho's Potato Expo, 1990 |

Notes:

- made by Pringles

| World's Largest Banana Split | 4.55 mi. long | NA | Selinsgrove, Pennsylvania, April 30, 1988 |

Notes:

- Assembled on town's Market Street

Food Item	Size	Ingredients	Where/ When Made
World's Largest Apple Pie	nearly 38,000 lbs.	32,000 lbs. apples, 7,000 lbs. flour and sugar	Wenatchee, Washington, 1997

Notes:
- had no top crust
- made by 300 volunteers at the North Central Washington Museum

World's Largest Cookie	20 tons, size of a basketball court	6,500 lbs. butter, 30,000 eggs, 5,000 lbs. sugar	North Carolina, June 2003

Notes:
- made as a fund-raiser for a Flat Rock, North Carolina, museum
- cost $10 a slice

Top Food-Related Crimes

The U.S., like virtually everywhere else in the world, is riddled with crime—so much so that the media is filled with stories of it and we viewers and readers are saturated by them. We've become jaded to crime—so much so that we decided to tickle that jaded palate by avoiding mention of run-of-the-mill crimes and focusing on a still understudied area of criminal behavior: crimes that do not involve a gun so much as a baked potato: your basic food-related crime.

BAT-JOGGER

Jim Schmitt of Wisconsin was jogging when it happened. His friend Todd Lenz spotted the creature first and shouted out a characteristic and accurate warning:

"Bat!" But it was too late. "Bam! Right in my face, and off it went," said Schmitt, who admitted he had been surprised to find a bat in his mouth. Regarding the taste of bat, he said, "It was real hard to get a real textured taste."

Just Follow That Meat-Juice Trail

That's what police in California did when called by a barbe-cuer in San Andreas who had been outdoors grilling a steak. She turned away, and when she turned back the steak was gone. Police explained the rest: "It had been stolen and a trail of meat juice was followed up to the next door apartment." Police deputies allegedly found the half-cooked steak in the bathroom and charged a woman there with receiving stolen property—namely, the steak.

Beer with a Vanilla Chaser

Want to buy some vanilla extract in Pennsylvania? Better show some ID. The problem is that vanilla extract can have as much alcoholic kick as vodka, and enterprising Pennsylvania thieves, realizing this, have been stealing it from supermarket shelves and getting drunk. So stores have been forced to remove it and place it behind the counters and have upped surveillance of the baking shelves.

Champagne Bandit

You've got to give him credit for discerning taste. This shoplifter stole only bottles of Moët & Chandon White Star champagne, from stores along Florida's Atlantic coast. Police were trying to get a motive, noting that the champagne is often served with cheese-based entrées, oysters, and fish. "Maybe he's a fine chef and he needs wine to accompany his meal," suggested a local police spokesman.

Smuggling . . . Cheese

It's a growing problem on the Mexican border with the U.S.; cheese smuggling. Customers buy white cheese in Mexico and sell it in Houston for a big profit, usually at flea markets. Customs officers say, "We find it everywhere—in car doors, boots, under the spare tire. It can be lucrative." How do officials usually find out which cars are carrying smuggled cheese? The smell. Particularly on hot Tex-Mex summer days.

Smuggling . . . Chocolate Eggs

Another cross-border smuggling problem, this time from north of the border. Kinder Surprise chocolate eggs have been banned in the U.S. due to potential choking hazards, so now people are ordering them via the Internet for three times the price—and smugglers are obliging by sneaking them into the U.S. One smuggler said, "It keeps growing and growing. I even have schools who order eggs in bulk."

Lobster Thieves

It was meticulously planned. A getaway car (actually, a getaway Chevy Blazer) was waiting. Jonathan Granger walked into a Red Lobster in Naples, Florida, went over to the lobster tank, reached in, and nabbed a live lobster. Cleverly concealing the clawed crustacean under his shirt, he made a run for it, to the getaway Blazer where his wife was waiting. The Blazer sped off. Unfortunately for the couple, alert wit-

★

EXCESSIVELY POPULAR ICE CREAM

New York City police in 2001 were beginning to wonder. There were *always* long lines of customers at a Brooklyn ice-cream truck—and not only on hot summer days. . . . And, oddly enough, the customers were mostly adults who seemed unusually . . . *intent* . . . on getting their ice cream.

Police finally moved in and found that the van was selling marijuana.

nesses noted the license number, and cops traced the lobster snatchers. Although Red Lobster offered to drop charges in exchange for payment for the lobster ($8.99), the couple was unrepentant: "This is a f***ing joke. We're in trouble for a f***ing $8.99 lobster?"

Crime with a Deadly Can of Ravioli

A man attempted to rob a store with a not-so-deadly weapon: a can of ravioli. The man allegedly walked into a corner store in Harrison Township, Pennsylvania, in 2001 and indicated to the clerk that he had something wrapped inside his shirt. He did—it was his can of ravioli. He so terrified the clerk that she couldn't get the cash register open; the man was later arrested when he tried to rob the local drugstore, using the same innovative ravioli technique.

Selling Counterfeit Veal

An upscale restaurant in San Jose, California, the Bella Mia, agreed to pay a $60,000 settlement for substituting pork in its veal dishes. A former chef confessed to the "crime" of making pork parmigiana and calling it veal parmigiana; in his defense, he said he thought pork was the superior meat.

Stupid Law and Lawyers in the U.S.A.

"The law is a ass."

So wrote Charles Dickens who, as we know, was not American but British.

But his words are applicable to the American legal system as well. Whether plaintiffs, defendants, or lawyers, those involved in American law manage all too well to make asses of themselves.

How Not to Impress the Legal System

Often, ordinary people wind up having to deal with the law. Perhaps it's a parking ticket or an unanswered jury summons. Small matters, usually. To ensure that they remain small, take the following as helpful hints on what one oughtn't do—examples of American brashness taken a bit too far.

Put excrement in your traffic-fine payment

Debra Angeline Schwarz of Lakeview, Oregon, sent in her $350 traffic fine and included what was called "a brown, pasty substance" in the envelope, later identified as human feces. "Everyone who had come in contact with the envelope testified that there was no doubt that the envelope was half-full of feces," said Lake County district attorney David Schutt. Schwarz was arrested on charges of criminal mischief, disorderly conduct, and obstructing government administration. In her defense, Schwarz claimed that she had asked someone else to mail the envelope—perhaps they had added the extra contents. She was found guilty on all counts.

Show up for your hearing wearing a kangaroo suit

Forty-year-old Daniel Kingery—who also happened to be a candidate for town selectman in Keene, New Hampshire—showed up in court wearing a costume that was half clown/half kangaroo. He was protesting what he considered discriminatory parking regulations, as the state allows people with disabled license plates to park at meters for free. He intentionally parked at expired meters over a few months, hoping to make his case. When called to appear at a hearing, he wore his costume to demonstrate that he felt it was a kangaroo court. The judge was not amused by his stance (or costume) and threatened him with contempt. (Note: Kingery, apparently a busy man, also appears below. . . .)

Use your jury summons as toilet paper— and then mail it in

Christopher Gurahian of Connecticut had been called for jury duty three times in two years. To demonstrate his feelings on this matter, he sent back his latest summons smeared with feces (officials were unsure whether they were human or animal, pending testing) with the words "stop wasting paper" written on it. To further clarify his feelings, on it he drew a stick figure of someone behind bars. Gurahian was charged with second-degree harassment and breach of peace.

(For judges only) Make flushing sounds in court with an amusing device designed for this purpose

Sheldon Schapiro, a Broward County, Florida, circuit judge has been accused of swearing at witnesses, berating lawyers, and using an electronic device that makes a toilet-flushing sound to convey his opinion of a defense lawyer's case. Among the specific allegations: He told a murder victim's mother who wanted to make a statement, "What do I need to hear from the mother of a dead kid for? All she will tell me is to keep the guy in custody and never let him out." The 65-year-old Schapiro has denied the allegations, while explaining that he used the toilet-flushing sound maker only once, during a rape case, and was merely intended as a "humorous comment."

Write profanity on the check you're using to pay a fine

Apparently a popular move but not one guaranteed to make friends and influence people. Judge John Pikkarainen of Howell, Michigan, does not look kindly on this self-expression. He sentenced one man who had done this to two days of community service, even though the man sent a one-and-a-half-page apology, and charged another (who had highlighted the obscene comment with a yellow marker) with contempt. Said the first offender: "I must say I would hesitate to write something so blunt on the check again, but I would definitely write something and choose my words carefully."

DON'T SWEAR TO THE DEAD
IN NORTH CAROLINA, NO SIR

Enough is enough, North Carolina legislators have said. It is now (as of June 2001) illegal to swear in front of dead bodies anywhere in the state of North Carolina. This clean-language law was already in effect for funeral homes—now it extends to everywhere a dead body is. This law comes with another proviso that the dead should be transported with some degree of dignity. This was found necessary after some bodies were found to have been carried with very little dignity—in the open back of a pickup truck.

Moon the judge

An East Texas man who had just been sentenced for aggravated assault decided to let the judge know just how he felt. Saying, "Hey, judge, look at this," he dropped his pants and mooned the judge, then the rest of the court. His self-expression garnered him an additional six months on his eight-year sentence.

Take off all of your clothes

William Parrish of Middletown, Ohio, was on trial for his role in a stolen-car chase when he took off all of his clothes. He refused to get dressed and was kicked out of the courtroom, the trial continuing without him. Sentenced to seven years, he tried to get a new trial, arguing that his constitutional rights were violated when he was told to leave. His appeal didn't work.

Great Moments in the Law

"I fought the law, and the law won" goes the song; but when you think about that song, and when you think about the "I" in that song, you usually picture some criminal or something. Or do you picture a Girl Scout? "The Girl Scout fought the law, and the law won?" Doesn't seem to fit.

Girl Scout troop nabbed by police

A small group of 8-year-old girls was nabbed early in 2001 for the crime of selling Girl Scout cookies in public, according to *The Atlanta Journal-Constitution*. After complaining to the officer, the kids waited for a sergeant to arrive; but when he did, he agreed: The Girl Scouts had broken the law. Finally, at the precinct house, the commander, Major Ron Slade, released the girls and apologized. "We love the Girl Scouts," he said. "I just bought some of their cookies."

13-year-old girl nabbed at metro station with stash of potato chips

A 13-year-old girl was nabbed at a metro station by police officers, arrested, and, of course, handcuffed. Then she was interrogated for two hours by police officers. Her crime? Munching on potato chips in the station. The girl was one of 12 children nabbed during a sweep of the station in Washington, D.C., a city with one of the highest murder rates in the nation—but now, thanks to vigilant officers under the direction of Police Chief Charles Ramsey and metro general manager Richard White, with one of the *lowest* potato-chip-consumption rates.

11-year-old faces the Big House

An 11-year-old boy from Staten Island is looking at some jail time—or at least a hefty fine—for ignoring jury-duty notices. No matter that he's got a number of years before he can legally serve on juries, that's too bad; if you ignore jury-duty notices, you go to jail for a month or pay $1,250. His father says he sent a copy of his son's birth certificate to officials, but they say they haven't seen it. And they need proof. County Clerk Stephen J. Fiala isn't taking no for an answer. "As soon as he gives me proof that his son is 11, I will remove him from the rolls." He adds, "You can't just call me up and say you're 11 years old. . . . The law mandates that I be given proof."

Elderly Cuban-American couple has home seized for holding poker games for friends and family

In 1999, a Miami couple had their $150,000 home seized by federal agents. Their crime: holding weekly poker games on their patio for friends and family. They got their house back . . . eventually . . . after an appeals court ruled the penalty was (a bit) "excessive."

Woman handcuffed and arrested for video-rental crime

It started with a routine traffic pull-over by New Hampshire cops for a broken taillight on Jessie Cohen's car. But during the license check, cops discovered that back in 1997 she had neglected to return a rented copy of the Woody Allen movie *Sleeper*. Cohen said she had no memory of having rented the video, nor did she remember receiving any overdue notices. No matter. She was handcuffed and charged with a misdemeanor: unauthorized use of rental property. And, of course, her Cadillac was impounded. A group championing individual rights summed up Cohen's case best: "You don't return a video on time and you get treated like Hannibal Lecter in *The Silence of the Lambs,* and end up starring in *Girls in Prison,* what sense does that make?"

McLawsuits: Supersized Awards for Superstupid Cases

A jury of our peers. To be tried by one is a right conferred upon American citizens by the Constitution. And, with typical American zeal, many of said peers go for the jugular when it comes to rewarding plaintiffs who seek to take on the Goliath corporations—or sometimes just the guy next door—regardless how dubious the merits of the case.

Some examples of the more generous juries and the more ridiculous lawsuits . . . in ascending order of payout:

$24,000: awarded to a San Francisco mugger
He sued a taxi driver who, seeing the mugging occur, captured him by pinning him against a building with his cab.

$2,699,000: awarded to a West Virginia convenience-store worker as punitive damages for injuring her back while struggling to open a pickle jar.
(She also received $130,066 in compensation and $170,000 for emotional distress.) State Supreme Court Justice Spike Maynard dissented from the ruling, calling the award "outrageous," so the court reviewed the case. In the end, the woman got a mere $2.2 million.

IN THE BELLY OF THE LAWSUIT:
Top 11 Stupid Lawsuits Filed by Inmates

When it comes to frivolous lawsuits, those that are often perhaps the most frivolous are those filed by inmates—who have more than the usual amount of time to kill. Reform legislation has cut back on the number of groundless inmate lawsuits, but they are still prevalent. Inmate lawsuits make up 25% of all civil suits in federal courts. In 2002, California spent $35 million on inmate lawsuits. Interestingly, of 30,000 inmate cases filed nationally, 28,000 of these were filed in New York State.

Should you wonder where some of your taxpayer money is going, herewith some of the more outrageous examples of grounds given for inmate lawsuits:

- toilet seat too cold

- prison didn't offer salad bars ($129 million)

- free-speech violation because prison guards disciplined inmate "for commenting on a guard's allegedly out-of-wedlock birth"

- while serving as an inmate-paralegal in the prison law library, was not paid the same wage that lawyers make

- gristle was found in turkey leg (this filed by a prisoner who has filed more than 140 actions in state and federal court)

- cruel and unusual punishment due to a limit on the number of Kool-Aid refills allowed

- unlawful discrimination on the basis of sex because Washington State would not allow a male inmate to transfer to an all-women correctional institution (filed by a prisoner who filed 184 actions in a little over three years)

- food was bad and portions too small (filed by an ex-chef in Oklahoma)

- a "defective" haircut resulted in lost sleep, headaches, and chest pains ($25,000)

- didn't receive scheduled parole hearing—while out on escape during the time of the hearing
- meal in "poor condition"—i.e., soggy sandwich and broken cookie

$8,000,000 (*divided between two people*): awarded to two professional carpet installers in Akron, Ohio.

Both sued the Para-Chem Company, manufacturers of carpet adhesive, after being severely burned in an explosion while using the product indoors. The adhesive had a warning label reading, "Do not use indoors because of flammability." But one juror said that he and his fellow jurors thought the warning label wasn't strong enough.

$14,100,000: awarded to a New York woman for injuries caused by a subway.

She was hit by it while lying on the tracks, attempting suicide.

Stupid Cases That Didn't Get the Payout

In the interest of evenhanded reporting, we should mention those cases in which the jury or judge was a bit more enlightened, shall we say—or, shall we say, not so stupid. Among the cases that didn't pay out:

$250,000,000: sought by David Kingery—a New Hampshire junkyard owner—for loss of a cultural facility.

Kingery sued the town of Peterborough in 1999 when

officials shut down the strip club that he operated at his junkyard. He claimed it was a cultural facility; the judge felt otherwise . . . and Kingery didn't collect.

$940,000: sought for injuries incurred while mooning through a third-story dorm window.

Former University of Idaho student Jason Wilkins climbed onto the heater in a room, mooned other students through the window . . . and then fell out. Wilkins sued the university, claiming that it had neither provided a safe environment for students nor had warned them strongly enough of the dangers of upper-story windows.

Unspecified high-six-figure dollar amount: **sought for not warning customers strongly enough about the dangers of eating while driving.**

William Bailey sued McDonald's after his car was rear-ended by another car at the drive-through window. The driver of the other car, John Parker, had gotten his food, put his burger and fries on the seat next to him and his chocolate milkshake between his legs. When Parker reached for his fries, he squeezed his legs together, causing the shake to spill onto his lap. Shocked by the cold, he hit the accelerator too hard, plowing into Bailey's car. Bailey sued both the driver and McDonald's, believing that McDonald's should warn its customers more strongly about the dangers of eating and driving. The judge was unimpressed by this novel claim and dismissed the case. (He did, however, also deny the McDonald's claim that Bailey should pay their attorney fees, stating that Bailey shouldn't be penalized for his creativity.)

Unspecified amount: **sought for emotional distress due to seeing one's mother getting wheeled into emergency surgery.**

In this twist on a malpractice case, sisters Janice Bird, Dayle Bird Edgmon, and Kim Bird Moran sued their mother's doctors and hospital after Janice took their mother, an ovarian cancer patient, to get a chemotherapy catheter inserted. But the procedure went wrong, and the mother was rushed into emergency surgery. Their complaint was not that their mother had received poor treatment (the surgery was successful) but that they were unduly distressed by seeing doctors rushing to help their mother.

The Jury Is Still Out

Since the wheels of justice never stop turning, following are several other rather *creative* cases that were still pending as of the writing of this book:

Complaint: not making the varsity basketball team
Amount sought: $1.5 million (plus firing of basketball coach)

Lynn Rubin filed on behalf of his son Jawann when he didn't gain a position on his high school varsity-basketball team. The complaint states that the family rearranged its schedules when the coach suggested Jawann try out for the varsity team. But Jawann didn't make the cut for varsity (according to the school, he was ineligible because he was a sophomore), and, after confronting his coach, he also was cut from the junior varsity. The dollar amount is optimisti-

AND THE KITCHEN SINK, TOO . . .

When Richard Espinosa of San Carlos, California, filed a suit because his dog had been attacked by a cat, he covered all—and we do mean all—bases. As specified in his 40-page claim, he sought damages for: "significant lasting, extreme and severe mental anguish" AND "emotional distress including, but not limited to, terror" AND "humiliation" AND "shame" AND "embarrassment" AND "mortification" AND "chagrin" AND "depression" AND "panic" AND "anxiety" AND "flashbacks" AND "nightmares" AND "loss of sleep" AND "loss of full enjoyment of life" AND "other physical and mental afflictions." Oh, and also pain and suffering. (Not surprisingly, Espinosa represented himself, as four lawyers declined.)

cally based on potential wages Jawann *could* have made as a professional ballplayer.

Complaint: not getting enough encouragement to lose weight and quit smoking

Amount sought: $1 million

Kathleen Ann McCormick of Wilkes-Barre, Pennsylvania, is asking for a tidy million from eight doctors at the Department of Veterans Affairs Medical Center as well as the U.S. government, which employs them, since she has had a heart attack and is now, as she terms it, a "cardiac invalid." McCormick, an overweight smoker with high blood pressure and cholesterol as well as a family history of heart disease, contends that the doctors "did not do enough" to get her to follow a more healthy lifestyle.

Complaint: emotional distress caused by being the "Winston Man"

Amount sought: $65 million

Raymond Leopard, the model who posed in Winston cigarette ads from 1978 to 1980, has sued R. J. Reynolds Tobacco for $65 million. His complaint isn't cancer or other illnesses suffered as a result of smoking Winstons (or any other cigarette), since Leopard says he didn't smoke. Rather, he is suing for the years of emotional distress he has suffered, caused by the guilt he feels from being a pawn in encouraging people to smoke.

Complaint: poor coaching
Amount sought: $700,000

A Middletown, Pennsylvania, teenager has filed suit against her softball coach, stating that his "incorrect" teaching style didn't allow her to develop as she should have as an athlete, thus resulting in her being unable to garner a college athletic scholarship.

Complaint: deceptive candlelike firecracker
Amount sought: $25,000

A Grand Haven, Michigan, woman has sued the owners of the condo she cleaned after she took a firecracker—which she mistook for a decorative candle. When she lit it later that night while at a restaurant, it exploded, injuring her. Her complaint: the condo owners shouldn't have left the firecracker where she could steal it without a warning on it. (The owners say that the ersatz candle looked like a "huge firecracker" and had been in a cupboard to keep it away from children.)

Complaint: defective pickle
Amount sought: $125,000

In another McDonald's case, a woman from Knoxville, Tennessee, is suing due to injuries from an "allegedly dangerous and defective product"—more specifically, a pickle. The hot pickle fell out of her burger, burned her chin, and caused her mental anguish. Her husband has also filed suit, citing the loss of "services and consortium of his wife."

Complaint: package created "impression of flimsiness"
Amount sought: Unspecified

The makers of Liquid Fire drain cleaner are being sued by a Georgia man because of injuries incurred . . . after he poured the contents into another bottle. He contends that the Liquid Fire bottle looked unsafe, so he felt compelled to transfer the liquid to his own container. In the process, he suffered chemical burns.

The Thirty Stupidest Warning Labels

Our litigious society has spawned not only wealth for many lawyers but also somewhat *different* (perhaps "eccentric" would be the better term) warning labels placed on products in possibly vain attempts to avoid lawsuits.

The group Michigan Lawsuit Abuse Watch even gives

BLOWING SMOKE

There have been a number of complaints and lawsuits concerning secondhand smoke but perhaps none as mind-boggling as this one: A Floridian filed a complaint with the state Division of Consumer Services, upset that he had been exposed to secondhand smoke. He had attended a live theater performance of Noel Coward's *Private Lives*—and the actors on stage had, as the script dictated, been smoking.

annual awards to the stupidest warning labels of the year (see www.mlaw.org). Herewith, then, some warning labels from recent years—from the banal to the baffling—that just may have saved companies from the rigors—and costs—of legalities . . . and certainly serve as testament to the awe-inspiring ingenuity of the American consumer:

Item	Warning
Toilet-bowl brush	Do not use orally
Snowblower	Do not use snowthrower on roof
Dishwasher	Do not allow children to play in the dishwasher
CD player	Do not use the Ultradisc2000 as a projectile in a catapult
Fireplace log	Caution—risk of fire
Birthday candles	Do not use soft wax as earplugs or for any other function that involves insertion in a body cavity
Electric router	This product not intended for use as a dental drill
Collapsible baby stroller	Remove child before folding
Sleeping pills	Warning: May cause drowsiness
Public toilet	Recycled flush water unsafe for drinking
Chainsaw	Do not attempt to stop chain with hands
Aim-n-Flame fireplace lighter	Do not use near fire, flame, or sparks
Underarm-deodorant can	Do not spray in eyes
Laser-printer toner	Do NOT eat toner
Iron	Never iron clothes while they are being worn
Hair dryer	Never use hair dryer while sleeping

Item	Warning
13-inch-wheel wheelbarrow	Not intended for highway use
Cardboard sunshield for car	Do not drive with sunshield in place
Hair dryer	Warning: Works on High Temperatures When Put on High Settings
Air conditioner	Do not place hand in fan while fan is running
Automotive air conditioner recycling machine	Suffocation may cause death
Window air conditioner	Warning: Do not allow air conditioner to fall out of window
Bathroom heater	This product is not to be used in bathrooms
Bicyclist's shin guards	Shin pads cannot protect any part of the body they do not cover
CD player	Warning—dangerous warning inside
Loop towel dispenser on Washington State ferries	Warning—do not put head inside towel loop
television-set manual	Do not pour liquids into your television set
TV remote control	Not dishwasher safe
Electric thermometer	Do not use orally after using rectally

Class-Action Suits

Perhaps it is a sign of the times. Perhaps it is a sign of the dollar. Regardless of the cause, class action suits are becoming more popular: filings increased by 338% in federal courts and by more than 1,000% from 1988 to 1998, and it appears that the increase will continue.

A class-action suit is a laudable thing: A company overcharges, scams, or otherwise harms unknowing consumers. Consumers band together (as a "class"), sue the company, and make it pay for its inequities. Lawyers are, of necessity, involved in said process. Such cases are most popular among personal-injury lawyers. Some members of a class might not be aware that they are actually participating, but this matters not to the intrepid justice-seeking lawyer—who, incidently, collects his or her usual contingency fee multiplied by the number of plaintiffs, aware or unaware as they may be.

So, yes, some lawyers are great believers in the power of the class-action suit. And for good reason, as the following suits may demonstrate. These are cases in which the justice of the class-action suit is a bit diminished . . . just as the payment to the lawyers is not:

Who Was Sued	What the Lawyer Received	What Each Class Member Received
Occidental Petroleum	$3 million	$0 (when one shareholder tried to protest the payout, he was informed by the lawyers that he couldn't appear in court as he had no stake in the settlement)
United Parcel Service	$8–$10 million	$0
General Mills, maker of Cheerios (sued due to a food additive—which wasn't harmful to consumers)	nearly $2 million	coupon for free box of Cheerios

Who Was Sued	What the Lawyer Received	What Each Class Member Received
Southwestern Bell (sued on behalf of 6 million consumers who had supposedly been exposed to misrepresentation of a service plan. The lawyer who filed the suit told the *Austin American-Statesman* that he actually had found little, if any, evidence of misconduct. The case was settled to avoid litigation costs)	$4 million	$15 credit on phone bill
Arista Records (sued when artists on their label, Milli Vanilli, were found to be lip-synching rather than singing on the *Girl You Know Its True* album)	$675,000 (the lawyers were not pleased with this amount and petitioned the court for an increase to $1.9 million)	$1–$3
The tobacco industry (sued by 60,000 non-smoking flight attendants. This was the first class-action lawsuit against the tobacco industry—and the first suit addressing secondhand smoke—to go to trial)	$49 million (of a $349 million award)	$0 (the other $300 million went to a foundation established to research second-hand smoke)

Who Was Sued	What the Lawyer Received	What Each Class Member Received
BancBoston Mortgage (sued to return funds held in escrow for mortgage customers)	$8.5 million	–$80–150 (–$91.13 on average) (yes, minus—class members had their accounts debited to pay for legal fees incurred fighting the suit)

Perhaps we are wrong, but there seems to be a trend here. . . .

Library Cop

You don't usually think of libraries when it comes to breaking the law. But maybe that's because we've got some tough cops and tougher librarians out there, ready and willing to stop library crimes at the outset.

The Case of the Missing Romance Novel

When LeRoy Anderson heard knocking and looked out and saw four police officers on his front step, he was worried—and puzzled. He couldn't think of a reason why the cops were there.

The cops could. They had come from 120 miles away to arrest him. His crime? Anderson had checked out two romance novels a year and a half before and had forgotten to return them. He tried to explain ("Listen, officer . . .")—he had moved and forgotten about the books—but the cops were, as cops should be, tough and unrelenting. Anderson was incarcerated until he paid his bail—and the library fine.

"Can you imagine going to jail over two books?" Anderson said. "You've got pedophiles and bank robbers out there, but they want to put me in jail for something that wasn't important enough to worry about several years ago."

Police Chief Richard Swartz doesn't see the point. "It's as bad or worse than speeding as far as I'm concerned," said the tough-on-books cop. "Too many people have a total disregard for public property."

The Case of the Dr. Seuss Book

In 1997, a 25-year-old Ann Arbor man had checked out a beloved Dr. Seuss book, his immortal *Green Eggs and Ham.* But he may have liked the book a little too much—because it was now 2001 and the book had still not been returned to the William P. Foust Public Library. Library officials alerted the police, who arrested the man for failing to appear in court to explain the missing book. The man posted bond and was released. Mark Raab of the Westland Police Department said, "Overall, it's kind of odd that you would arrest someone for not returning books. But I guess the library has to do what it has to do. . . ."

The Case of the Four Overdue Notices

Nolan County-City Library isn't kidding around. The tough librarians of Sweetwater, Texas, are issuing arrest warrants for library patrons after four notices—four notices and you're out! The warrant, for theft of services, carries a maximum penalty of six months in jail and a $2,000 fine.

The Case of the Overdue Dolphin Book

When the 12-year-old returned her overdue library book on dolphins and paid the fine, she thought her troubles were over. But the wheels of the law grind exceedingly slow and exceedingly fine. She was now ordered to go to the Littleton (Colorado) Municipal Court to answer a legal summons regarding the book. She was required to show the judge her library receipts and pay a $15 fee to have the case dismissed. The girl's mother hoped that her daughter could avoid court. "It's appalling that we can't even send a child to the library without having to worry about something like this," she said. But at least for the librarians, there may be a happy ending: Apparently, the girl is now too scared to go again to the library, so they won't have to worry about any more overdue books from at least one miscreant.

Stupid Money and Stocks in the U.S.A.

No, money isn't everything. But money—making it and spending it—has been important in America from the time the first European settlers arrived. The earlier Indian inhabitants managed to make do quite nicely without the almighty dollar, as unimaginable as this must seem. Indeed, our Indian predecessors were no doubt surprised to find odd-looking white-skinned Europeans with excessive amounts of facial hair confidently setting specific monetary values on various chunks of real estate—"Hmm, yes, that island there is worth $24 and change. The river, $14 exactly, or 10 dollars in gold." The concept must have seemed absolutely ludicrous and hardly civilized. Doesn't the land belong to all? Like the water and the sky? In a word, no. Not now. The Europeans felt they knew better, and they knew that valuation is primarily monetary and preferably in thalers, dollars, or British sterling (although they may have entertained other valuation theories during the hour or so spent on their end-of-the-week holy ministrations).

And so, ever since, making and spending money has been a great American pastime, pursued with that great abundance of innocent and energetic enthusiasm that makes us truly American. Sometimes, of course, that innocent, wonderful American enthusiasm can be a bit excessive, a bit overreaching, and the pursuit of money can result in situations that we may review with disgust, disdain, and amusement. . . .

Standard Normal Greedy CEO Section

You will be confronted with questions every day that test your morals. Think carefully and, for your sake, do the right thing, not the easy thing.

> —Dennis Kozlowski, then CEO of Tyco, now under investigation for billion-dollar fraud, indicted for conspiring to avoid sales taxes, and accused by shareholders of massive wasting of corporate money

For many CEOs, the right thing, not the easy thing, appears to be amassing millions of dollars' worth of knickknacks, vacation homes, and the like for personal use . . . on the company's dollar. Perhaps the rationale is that a superrich and happy CEO makes for happy profits. Then again, how much in the way of profits did Enron or WorldCom, whose CEOs are represented here, actually make?

Are we being cynical?

How Much Shareholder Money CEOs Spent for Personal Junk

Cost	What the Money Bought	Who Bought It
$445	pincushion	Dennis Kozlowski, CEO, Tyco
$2,900	wastepaper basket	Dennis Kozlowski, CEO, Tyco
$6,000	designer shower curtain	Dennis Kozlowski, CEO, Tyco

Cost	What the Money Bought	Who Bought It
$6,300	sewing-basket end table	Dennis Kozlowski, CEO, Tyco
$15,000	umbrella stand (in defense, Wendy Valliere, Kozlowski's interior decorator, said, "It's not just some stupid dog umbrella stand. It's a very unique, beautiful" umbrella stand)	Dennis Kozlowski, CEO, Tyco
$17,000	toiletries case	Dennis Kozlowski, CEO, Tyco
$20,000 per month	rent on apartment at Waldorf-Astoria Towers, New York City	Leo Hindery, former CEO, Global Crossing (sued the company for failing to meet the terms of his severance agreement, which included this perk. Meanwhile, 5,000 were left jobless by Global Crossing's collapse)
$100,000	gift to wife	Dennis Kozlowski, CEO, Tyco
$100,000	gift to mistress	Dennis Kozlowski, CEO, Tyco
$200,000	assorted baubles at Tiffany	Dennis Kozlowski, CEO, Tyco
$347,600	apartment rent	Dennis Kozlowski, CEO, Tyco
$590,000	vinyl sculptured light switch	Lea Fastow, wife of ex-Enron CFO Andrew Fastow
$5 million	oceanfront estate in Nantucket	Dennis Kozlowski, CEO, Tyco
$7.4 million	expense account: living and personal relocation expenses	Mark Frevert, chairman, Enron Wholesale Services
$12.8 million	golf course	John Rigas, CEO, Adelphia
$14 million	loan to buy ski chalet in Park City, Utah	Mark Belnick, chief legal counsel, Tyco

Cost	What the Money Bought	Who Bought It
$14 million	furnishings and renovation for houses	Dennis Kozlowski, CEO, Tyco
$24 million	two New York City apartments	Dennis Kozlowski, CEO, Tyco
$29 million	Boca Raton, Florida, house	Dennis Kozlowski, CEO, Tyco
$41.66 million	Gulfstream V jet (company owned but for personal use only—for such things as reportedly carting some of his daughter's personal furniture, including a queen-size bed, to France and back)	Ken Lay, chairman, Enron
$70 million	loans	Ken Lay, chairman, Enron
$250 million	margin calls on personal stock account	John Rigas, CEO, Adelphia
$408 million	loans	Bernie Ebbers, CEO, WorldCom
$3.1 billion	loan (from which spent $150 million spent on Buffalo Sabres hockey team; $13 million for backyard golf course; $700,000 for country-club membership)	John Rigas, CEO, Adelphia

Truly Golden Retirement Package

During his last year at General Electric, CEO Jack Welch earned $16.2 million. He also held 22 million shares which, at about $28 a share, were worth approximately $616 million.

Evidently, this was not enough.

Prior to leaving, Welch negotiated for more. Much more. Such as the following GE shareholder–provided perks:

- $9 million annual pension
- Central Park apartment (estimated value of $80,000 a month), complete with flowers, food, satellite TV, and so on
- limited-edition 2003 Mercedes-Benz SLR
- twenty-four-hour access to a Boeing 737 owned by GE (valued at $291,869 a month, according to an expert hired by Mrs. Welch)
- cellular phones for five cars
- five computers, complete with technical support
- initiation and dues for Augusta, Pine Valley, Blind Brook, and other country clubs
- financial-planning and tax services
- lifetime box-seat tickets to Yankee Stadium (the box behind the Yankees dugout) *and* Fenway Park
- VIP tickets to NBC entertainment, news, and sports events (which includes Red Sox games, the Metropolitan Opera, and others)
- French Open tickets (VIP seating)
- U.S. Open tickets (courtside seating)
- Wimbledon tickets (VIP seating)
- $86,000 annual retainer (for five days of work per year)

Interestingly, the charitable-donations listing in Welch's GE benefits program is $100,000, with the company providing a matching donation of $100,000—0.00625% of his last year's income.

Welch was initially angry when details of his package were revealed . . . and reviled: "In today's reality, my 1996 employment contract could be misportrayed as an excessive retirement package, rather than what it is—part of a fair employment and post-employment contract made six years ago."

Perhaps others disagreed. Once it reached the public light, the package was revised. Welch agreed to give up most of those benefits and pay his former employer $2.5 million per year for the perks.

How to Be a Greedy Capitalist Pig (and Screw Your Employees and the Stockholders at the Same Time): The Enron Story

Americans love a winner, and we can argue that Enron was one. It was number one.

The problem, of course, is that this number one refers to bankruptcy. Enron was the largest bankruptcy in America.

Before achieving number one, Enron was number seven. It was America's seventh-largest company; it employed 21,000 people in more than 40 countries; it was busy making fortunes for stockholders, employees, and top executives. Especially for top executives. Top executives like chairman Ken Lay and CEO Jeff Skilling—who got raises. Healthy raises. Lay got a $153 million raise. Skilling didn't fare as well—his raise was only $127 million.

Enron was, or seemed to be, a great success story. An energy firm that traded energy futures, it in effect made the energy business more like the stock market. It was revolutionary, it was sexy, it was the "World's Coolest Company—that's what we all felt was probably a better description," Skilling said. "Ken [Lay] even said, 'Maybe we get some giant sunglasses and put 'em around the outside of the building.' "

It was superprofitable, and it was the American dream personified—or, rather, corporatized. Except, of course, that maybe, just maybe, it wasn't true. An awful lot of the profits Enron reported—in fact, maybe even all of the profits it reported—were kind of . . . fake. Apparently, instead of really working buying and selling energy, many Enron top executives were busy doing other things, like:

- falsifying records
- concealing company debt
- misleading analysts
- reporting nonexistent profits
- avoiding taxes
- creating a cutthroat, no-questions-asked working environment.

But before saying more, let's throw in a few adverbs about Enron: allegedly, perhaps, maybe. We must be careful. All of this is still in the courts. Let's just say this: Andrew Fastow, the former chief financial officer of Enron, has been charged with not one, not two, but with 78 counts of fraud, money laundering, conspiracy, and other charges a bit more serious than jaywalking. Are these charges simply examples of government prosecutorial excess and lurid governmental fantasies?

Maybe.

But let's not bet on it.

Enron Fast 'n' Fun Facts

- Enron is the only company in the world to have its own Amnesty International report due to reports of worker mistreatment at their $3 billion power plant in Dahbol, India.

- Enron paid not one cent of income tax from 1996 to 1999.

- Good excuse department: Jeff Skilling, a former CEO of Enron, claimed he was unable to remember anything about a directors' meeting in which were approved a number of multimillion-dollar partnership deals that were allegedly fraudulent. Why couldn't he remember? Because "the room was dark, quite frankly, and people were walking in and out of the meeting." (He said "I do not recall" 26 times during the congressional hearing.)

- A line from the Enron employee manual on "Business Ethics": "Moral as well as legal obligations will be fulfilled openly, promptly, and in a manner which will reflect pride on the Company's name."

- And . . . a line from the "Who We Are" section of their website: "It's difficult, too, to talk about Enron without using the word innovative. Most of the things we do have never been done before."

- Crying on TV, possibly in a bid for sympathy (or is that being uncharitable?), Linda Lay, wife of Ken Lay, pleaded poverty, sobbing, "Everything we had was mostly in Enron stock. . . . We are struggling for liquidity." She failed to mention that the Lays at that moment owned $8 million worth of stock in other corporations and $25 million in real estate.

- Enron's accountant during its run was the once venerable firm of Arthur Andersen. Andersen verified the books, making sure that when Enron claimed a profit, there really was a profit. Needless to say, it doesn't appear that Andersen did its job all that well. But let's give it credit for chutzpah. In June, shortly after resigning from his post as CEO of Arthur Andersen, Joseph Berardino arrived in Palo Alto to deliver a lecture on . . . reforming the accounting industry. Berardino told the San Jose *Mercury News* that he was "in a unique position" to discuss the matter.

A Ken Lay moment

As Enron was collapsing and employees were being laid off, top executives thought about how much to pay them. Given the state of corporate finances, they found it difficult to exceed a $13,500 payout per employee; in fact, they paid that amount only after ex-employees forced them into court. However, these same executives did manage to scrape the bottom of the barrel and come up with a little bit for themselves: $67 million for chairman Ken Lay, $33.5 million for Mark Frevert, and $40 million for CEO Jeff Skilling. Ex-workers at Enron weren't pleased. Sandra Stone, a former executive assistant, complained, "I have lost my entire friggin' retirement to these people. They have raped us all."

Harsh words.

The good Mr. Lay's response? Kelly Kimberley, Mr. Lay's assistant, reported that Mr. Lay was "deeply saddened by the impact the Enron collapse has had on current and former employees and shareholders. He's a strong believer in God and believes everything will work out."

CHEERING THE ENRON TROOPS WITH T&A

We look at this as something to heighten the hearts of Enron employees who are losing their jobs.

—*Playboy* spokeswoman Elizabeth Norris, commenting on the magazine's Women of Enron issue

Our Favorite "Get the Corporate Loot" Excuse

In April 2002, a proxy statement for the company E-Trade showed the payout—or, to put it in corporate terms, the compensation package—for Christos Cotsacos, the CEO. His salary was listed as $4.9 million; he was given $29 million in stock options; and, oh, yes, that $15-million-dollar loan made by the company? Forget about it—don't bother paying it back. This enormously high compensation was justified by a spokesperson for the company: "It reflects the success the company has had under his leadership." For the record, the company lost $241 million—and, eight months later, Cotsacos himself, who resigned.

The Wall Street Hall of Shame: The Stupidest Advice from Stock Analysts

Here's one of those great, easy ways to make money: Tell people to buy a stock and . . . as it goes down, keep on telling them to buy it. Meanwhile, collect $10 or $20 million in salary. Some people in the 1990s got jobs like this; for some arcane reason, they were called stock "analysts." If they had

HOW TO HAVE YOUR CAKE AND EAT IT TOO . . .

Corporations like Enron, MCI, and Qwest Communications that are under investigation for inflating their earnings (and thereby reaping the rewards of investor confidence and high stock prices) have figured out a clever way to find a silver lining in that cloud. . . . Now that the Feds are making them come clean and admit lower earnings, they're filing for tax refunds based on those lower earnings.

used a dartboard instead of "analyzing," average investors who listened to them might have been considerably better off.

Some of their names will live on forever: Grubman, Blodgett, Meeker—purveyors of some of the worst stock advice in history, if we argue that good stock advice helps the consumer make money. Together, some of these analysts have perhaps helped more people lose more money on the exchanges than ever before in history. It's no wonder one of them, Grubman, keeps an armed guard at his side. Such dismal stock-picking records do not inspire great love from clients—the proverbial widows, orphans, old pensioners, and average people who have lost a lot. But then again, it's not just the analyst's fault. Wall Street lives by telling you to buy stocks, not to sell them. Just recently, there were 8,000 stock-analyst recommendations on Wall Street. Of those, 29 were sell recommendations: less than one half of 1 percent. Here are some of the dud picks from some "top" analysts of the great stock boom:

Dud Stock: Priceline.com
Who Picked It: Mary Meeker (Morgan Stanley)

Priceline.com was Mary Meeker's most inspiring stock pick. While her firm, Morgan Stanley, was making millions in fees raising money for Priceline.com, Mary's bold independent analysis of the stock concluded that—it was a real buy!

She wasn't influenced at all by the fact that her employer's investment wing preferred that she recommend the stock. We can be sure of this, because Mary said so and the government has since agreed. "We maintain a strict separation of the [investment] banking and research functions within the firm. Our research is objective and long-term," she once explained.

It was certainly long-term. Mary recommended the stock and kept on touting it for the long haul—all the way down. First, she recommended the stock at $134 a share. Then, in April 1999, at $104. Soon afterward, shares tumbled. At $78 a share, Meeker put the stock under her keen eye—and repeated her recommendation. Buy! Priceline. com fell some more. At $3 a share, Meeker examined the company again and concluded that it was . . . a real buy.

Proverbial Widow Meter: What a $10,000 investment would be worth if a proverbial widow had put her money in Priceline.com from the beginning (reflecting the 1 for 6 split) to mid-2003: $274.62

Dud Stock: Amazon.com (not so dud now, but a real dud at $400)

Who Picked It: Henry Blodgett (Merrill Lynch)

Henry gave the world a phrase: "to Blodgett" a stock means to tout it to the moon even if it belongs underground. And "Blodgett" is just what Henry did with Amazon.com.

He thought of this all back when Amazon.com stock was

selling at about $243 a share. After some brilliant analysis, Henry concluded it would go up to $400, even though the company hadn't yet made a profit. Lo and behold, it did go up, and Henry was a genius. Almost everyone except true ace stock picker Warren Buffett said so.

Problem was Henry couldn't stop. He recommended the stock all the way up . . . and pretty much all the way down. During Henry's period of buy recommendations, Amazon lost 75% of its value. And along the way, Henry got into a little trouble: It seemed that all the while he was recommending some other Internet stocks to outsiders, he was trashing them via e-mails to friends, using some really nasty language. Merrill Lynch was "shocked, shocked" by such unusual unethical behavior.

Proverbial Widow Meter: What $10,000 would be worth if a proverbial widow put her money in Amazon during Blodgett's touting of the stock: $2,500

Dud Stock: Pets.com
Who Picked It: Henry Blodgett (Merrill Lynch)

Here's another Henry winner. Pets.com was an Internet pet store with a cool sock puppet mascot. Pets.com's financing was arranged by Merrill Lynch, and of course we can be sure that Henry picked it as a hot stock only by coincidence.

The idea was simple: Buy your pet supplies online. It was a good idea, but only a few customers liked it. And customers, remember, are what really count.

But Henry must not have noticed. He made a buy recommendation at $16. When Pets.com started having a few problems and the stock fell to $7, Henry looked it over and concluded: buy. What about when it fell to $2? Henry thought and said, "Buy." A little later, at $1.69? Buy. Finally, at $1.43 Henry changed his recommendation, not to "sell" but to "accumulate."

Pets.com got hard to accumulate not long after that, since it was kicked off the stock exchange. Not so long afterward, Henry was kicked off, too.

Proverbial Widow Meter: What $10,000 would be worth if a proverbial widow put her money in Pets.com from the beginning: roughly, $0.00

Dud Stock: WorldCom

Who Picked It: Jack Grubman (Salomon Smith Barney)

Jack, formerly of Salomon Smith Barney, is a genius, if he says so himself.

In fact, many sources say he sort of did. It seems that Jack's claim that he attended MIT wasn't quite true, nor did he pull himself up by his own bootstraps out of the gritty streets of South Philly. Jack explained that all by saying he "probably felt insecure" when he lied or whatever not quite telling the truth is called on Wall Street. But that's all behind us now.

In 2001, Jack issued a 28-page report modestly called "Grubman's State of the Union," in which he picked ten companies and said that in 12 to 18 months investors would look back and wished they'd picked them, too. Of the 10 companies this non-MITer picked, 5 soon afterward traded below $1 a share, and 3 filed for bankruptcy. Way to go, Jack!

But Jack is most famous for his dealings with the telephone company WorldCom, which he claimed to know a lot about; he boasted he had an insider's view of the company, which we should hope for his sake isn't true because a lot of bad things happened there that shouldn't have, some of which were quite possibly illegal. But that's for the courts to decide.

Jack recommended WorldCom stock at a high of $64.50 and then at progressively lower increments as the stock began to sink. At $29 or so, when investors were more than a little worried, Jack explained to all those "Nervous Nellies" that the value of all the wires and switches that World-Com owned was about $25 per share, so the stock really couldn't go down much farther. Too bad! Jack was wrong, it went down to almost zero; all those wires and switches weren't considered to be worth so much after all. Still, as one Salomon Smith Barney executive explained, Jack saved his followers a lot of money in the end: He recommended selling the stock at about $2, just before it went down to $1. Grubman saved his customers 50% of their money!

Proverbial Widow Meter: What $10,000 would be worth if a proverbial widow put her money in WorldCom from the "buy" high to the "sell" recommendation: $310.07

Dud Stock: Global Crossing
Who Picked It: Jack Grubman (Salomon Smith Barney) Jack loved this stock, too.

Global Crossing was going to lay fiber-optic cables and pipes all over America then all over the world. And Jack was in on it at the beginning; he advised the company on some takeover bids, and between September 1998 and June 2001 he issued 16 buy recommendations on the stock.

Problem was, the stock, after going up to $61.38 in 1999, started going down pretty steadily after that; very steadily down, in fact. Way down, to put it more accurately. Jack told everyone not to panic, for heaven's sake, Global Crossing was a new breed of tech firm that was well funded—and after all, he should know. Finally, after Global Crossing went through five CEOs in four years and announced a not-so-pretty business model, even Jack got worried and decided maybe investors shouldn't buy the stock after all. He cut his recommendation to neutral.

But now, the stock was at . . . $1. Thanks, Jack! And soon afterward, the company filed for bankruptcy (the fourth-largest Chapter 11 bankruptcy ever), and Jack issued a very terse statement saying he had stopped covering the stock. It didn't matter. No one was covering the bankrupt stock until it got reorganized.

Proverbial Widow Meter: What $10,000 would be worth if a proverbial widow put her money in Global Crossing from the beginning: $0.00

The Wonderful World of Wall Street: Great Moments in Stock-Market Mistakes

Investment firm Bear Stearns made a little mistake on October 2, 2002. They were supposed to place orders to sell $4 million worth of stocks. Instead, due to a clerical error, they sold 1,000 times that amount. A spokesman said the company recovered about 85% of the sold stock, losing a mere 152 times what they intended, and added that it would have no significant impact on the company. Pouring salt to the wound, the early edition of *The Wall Street Journal* the next day contained a story about the mistake near a Bear Stearns ad that boasted of the firm's ability to "execute complex transactions flawlessly." The story was moved to a less embarrassing spot in later editions.

TO PROTECT THE INTERESTS OF YOU, THE LITTLE CONSUMER

The New York Stock Exchange appoints "public" representatives—people who oversee the exchange to see that it truly works for the public good.

As of 2003, the public representatives dedicated to the little average investor included Mel Karmazin (COO of the small multibillion-dollar company Viacom), Juergen Schrempp (CEO of one of the smaller of the international car companies, DaimlerChrysler), Carlo Bartze (CEO of the software maker Autodesk, which is a lot smaller than Microsoft), William Harrison (CEO of the smaller multinational bank JP Morgan Chase), Gerald Levin (former CEO of Time Warner—he probably is a fair pick, since he made Time Warner a much smaller company during his tenure as CEO, losing it billions of dollars), and Carl McCall (a public servant and new member of the board of Tyco, a multinational earlier accused of massive fraud).

Average investors will also be pleased to note that the low-level multimillionaire Martha Stewart was also a public representative until she resigned last year after allegations of stock fraud.

The Rich Are Different. . . . : Gross (and Stupid) Excess in America

Many Americans want to be rich. This explains the popularity of Lotto, Powerball, and casinos. But what of those of us who haven't pillaged a company, married and divorced a wealthy spouse, or won Lotto?

Unfortunately, there is little one can do. It appears that funds are necessary to be rich. But perhaps the following might lend ideas on how, at least, to fake it.

How to Be a Wealthy Party Giver

When planning a 40th birthday party that costs $2.1 million (half of which will be picked up by your company), it is important to overlook no small detail. The following e-mail from a Tyco staffer to the party planners (as reproduced at www.thesmokinggun.com) gives us insight into this. The party in question: one given at a Sardinian resort for Tyco CEO Dennis Kozlowski's wife, Linda (a former waitress at a restaurant near Tyco headquarters). Note the tasteful use of an ice sculpture of Michelangelo's David.

> *Guests arrive at the club starting at 7:15 p.m. The van pulls up to the main entrance. Two gladiators are standing next to the door, one opens the door, the other helps the guests. We have a lion or horse with a chariot for the shock value. . . . We have gladiators standing guard every couple feel [sic] and they are lining the way. The guests come into the pool area, the band is playing, they are dressed in elegant chic. Big ice sculpture of David, lots of shellfish and caviar at his feet. A waiter is pouring stoli [sic] vodka into his back so it comes out his penis into a crystal glass.*

How to Be a COST-CUTTING Socialite

Even millionaires aren't impervious to the need to cut costs. Their method of cutting back, however, does not entail clipping coupons. Rather, it is a more complicated affair.

Herbert Black, a personal financial adviser to socialite Denise Rich (ex-wife of financier Marc Rich), sued her for nonpayment of fees. He claimed he had saved her almost $1 million a year by instituting certain cost-effective measures. Among them:

- $125,000 saved in flowers, by arranging to have fewer deliveries to her apartment when she wasn't at home

- $30,000 saved by changing the payment plan for her yoga lessons

- $52,000 saved in "dog maintenance" (which included giving away her two oldest dogs, who, unable to walk well, had been pushed by dog-sitters around Central Park in an $8,000 baby carriage).

How to Be a Billionaire's Kid

Being a billionaire's child carries with it the need for money to maintain a lifestyle necessary for a billionaire's child (even at age 3).

Let us take a look at Kira Kerkorian, 3-year-old daughter of 84-year-old billionaire Kirk Kerkorian. Or rather, let us take a look at a few of the monthly expenses incurred by the girl, according to papers filed by her mother, Lisa Bonder Kerkorian, during a battle over child-support payments. The amount sought: $323,000 a month (or $3.88 million annually) as "what is required to maintain her in the station of life and with all the things and benefits befitting the daughter of Kirk Kerkorian." (Kira's first birthday party cost $70,000.)

- $144,000 travel expenses
- $16,704 lawyers' fees
- $14,083 parties and play dates
- $7,000 charity (Kira is apparently a generous 3-year-old)
- $4,300 food (eaten in home)

- $5,900 food (eaten out of home. Note: This includes food eaten by nannies or friends)
- $3,386 French/ballet/tennis/piano/riding lessons
- $2,500 clothing and shoes
- $2,500 movies, theaters, and "outings"
- $1,416.67 gifts "to and from Kira"
- $1,400 laundry and cleaning
- $1,000 toys, videos, and books
- $436 care for pet bunny

How to Be a Rich Drunk

Order a drink at the World Bar (in New York City's new Trump World Tower). More specifically, order their special $50 cocktail, which includes Remy XO, Pineau des Charentes, freshly pressed grapes, Veuve Clicquot champagne, and a bit of liquid gold.

How to Be a Rich Person's Pet

Pets of the rich and famous are a pampered lot. Rather than be stuck in a kennel while its owners are away, a wealthy person's pet can be taken care of in the manner to which it is accustomed, which is to say better than the average person.

Upscale pet hotels have opened in New York, Hollywood, and Fairfax County, Virginia (near Washington, D.C.), charging prices of more than $200 a day and offering perks that would please the most pampered of pooches. Among them:

- hydrotherapy pool
- state-of-the-art exercise room
- beauty salon

- suites with satellite TV, classical music, and original artwork

How to Be a Rich, Car-Loving Comedian

What does one do when one owns a number of vintage cars and also lives in New York City, which is not known for its accessible parking.

This was the plight faced by comedian Jerry Seinfeld. So, one of his companies bought a two-story building on West 83rd Street for $880,000 in cash, to convert it to a garage.

Among the amenities planned upon completion of a $500,000 gut renovation:

- terrazzo floors
- wood paneling
- heating/air-conditioning system
- stainless-steel shelving and cabinet storage systems
- skylight
- office on top floor (844 square feet)
- modern glass and metal staircase
- kitchenette
- bathroom with shower
- outdoor deck
- heavy-duty elevator for moving cars between cellar and ground floor

This is not to say this is necessarily the garage of one's dreams. The space (16 by 52 feet) will probably hold only about 20 cars.

The Rich and Their Ranches

This is a new spin on the time-honored "I'm an old cow-hand" spirit. Multimillionaire corporate CEOS or celebrities buy thousands of acres to get back to the land. The key to doing this well is to be megawealthy, buy thousands of acres then "play" a little with your ranch, and get federal money in assistance. And you should also remember that a working ranch is a tax write-off.

How much can you get? Most of the federal government's subsidies. Almost two thirds of the $27 billion in federal farm subsidies paid in 2001 went to just 10 percent of America's farm owners, including multimillion-dollar corporations and multimillionaires.

Some prime examples of how to be a so-called Rolex rancher (best perused while humming "I'm an Old 'Filthy Rich' Cowhand"):

Collect healthy federal subsidies even if you are worth many billions

Cases in point: "Cowboy" David Rockefeller (former Chase Manhattan Bank chairman; grandson of oil tycoon John D. Rockefeller) owns 300 acres in upstate New York. His net worth: approximately $2.5 billion. In spite of this, to help run the ranch he has collected federal assistance: USDA subsidy payments (1996–2001) of $494,451—$134,557 for 2001 alone.

Similarly, "Cowboy" Ted Turner hasn't turned his nose up at subsidies, accepting about $190,000 in 2000 to help defray the costs of his 15 different ranches. (As of 1996, he owned 1.6% of New Mexico.) Russ Miller, manager of Turner's farm and ranch companies, based in Bozeman,

Montana, said more than half the subsidies his boss got were for conservation programs. He added that Turner has spent millions of his own money on such projects. "We feel there is a public good from what we are doing on our farmland," Miller said.

Take advantage of public grazing lands even if you are worth many, many millions

Case in point: "Cowboy" Barron Hilton, chairman of the Hilton hotel chain, owner of the Flying M Ranch, near Carson City, Nevada, and of more than 450,000 acres (which includes both private and public lands). Hilton's net worth is estimated at $500 million. Yet he frugally takes advantage of public grazing lands, for which he pays $1.35 per cow per month to the government for the cattle to graze on public land. This is compared to the more than $11 each it would cost to graze on private land.

Get whatever possible tax write-off you can under the guise of protecting land

Case in point: "Cowboy" Michael Jackson, singer and owner of the infamous Neverland Ranch. By taking advantage of tax breaks, he has been able to pay only about $13,000 in property tax (on property assessed at nearly $12.3 million), rather than more than $6 million without the tax break. Problem is, Jackson can develop only two of the ranch's acres for nonagricultural uses in order to claim the major tax breaks. Santa Barbara zoning officials say he has used three times that amount. The ranch includes a guardhouse, recreational buildings, barns, a playground, and amusement rides.

If accepting subsidies, don't let the press hear too much about it (especially if you are a member of the press)

Case in point: Sam Donaldson, ABC News newscaster (who reportedly earns at least $2 million year in salary and also pulls in about $30,000 per lecture), owner of 27,000 acres in Hondo, New Mexico, 1,300 sheep, and nearly 300 cattle. Donaldson initially saw the ranch as his "getting in touch with the people" move, saying in a 1994 *Columbia Journalism Review* article, "I'm trying to get a little ranching business started in New Mexico. I've got five people on the payroll. I'm making out those government forms [which] gives me something to be in touch with America about." He also got in touch with federal subsidies. In fact, according to USDA data, he was the third-largest recipient of wool and mohair payments in Lincoln County, getting $97,000 in subsidy checks over the period 1993–1995 (sent to his address in the Virginia suburbs of Washington, D.C.). He also got free help from the Animal Damage Control Program, which allowed him to call USDA agents to his ranch 412 times over five years in order to kill 74 coyotes and 3 bobcats that were preying on his livestock, at a cost of roughly $100,000 to taxpayers. After 1996, he stopped accepting subsidies, presumably because of the media attention he received.

If possible, have your company foot the bill for your ranch

Case in point: "Cowboy" Bernie Ebbers, former CEO of WorldCom who owned the Douglas Lake Ranch (Canada's largest ranch), which had cost him a cool $67 million. (The ranch was recently sold by WorldCom in an effort to recoup some of the more than $400 million in loans owed by him.) This down-home ranch has a staff of 75 (including 15 real cowboys) and is said to turn a profit as it sells cattle and timber and also hosts social events such as weddings. (Wedding parties can opt for one of two different meal plans: BBQ-beef sandwiches at a mere $13.95 a head or BBQ-steak dinner at $21.95 a head.)

The Poor Can't Win

- Average fine levied by the Environmental Protection Agency for hazardous-waste violations in white neighborhoods: $335,566

  Average fine in minority neighborhoods: $55,318

- Chances of an audit in 2002 by the IRS if you're a member of the "working poor": 1 in 174

  Chances of an audit in 2002 by the IRS if you're poor and claimed an earned-income tax credit: 1 in 64

  Chances of an audit by the IRS if you make more than $100,000: 1 in 208

Stupid Taxes
in the U.S.A.

Taxes. One of those two inevitabilities in life (the other being, of course, death). As one might suspect, taxes are a rich source of American stupidity—both on the side of the IRS and on the side of the average taxpayer.

"We Want to Be People-Friendly": Heartwarming Examples of the IRS in Action

The Internal Revenue Service is not well known in our Land of the Free as one of the friendlier government agencies; in fact, the "Service" in their name sounds more Orwellian and sinister than anything else. Hence, when the IRS decided recently to refurbish its image, most people took the idea with a large grain of salt. A wise move, particularly as these heartwarming examples of the new, kinder, gentler IRS so readily show.

IRS demands money up front from terrorism victims

The family of Lockerbie terrorist victim Mark Zwynenburg received a bill from the IRS for $6,484,339.39; this is based on the fact that the Zwynenburg family had sued Pan Am for $11,000,000 in damages. The facts that Pan Am is bankrupt and the Zwynenburgs haven't received a cent didn't matter: The IRS demanded its cut of the money up front, ordering the Zwynenburgs to pay up within 90 days.

IRS charges man for underpaying taxes by a penny

George Wittemeier was penalized $159.78 for underpaying his taxes by one cent.

IRS sends taxpayer bill for $68 billion

In the 1990s, a 36-year-old Centerville, Virginia, systems engineer, already paying $500 a month for a past IRS debt, received an updated bill for $68 billion. The engineer's biggest surprise came when he called the IRS to ask what was going on: "I talked to several people who didn't think it was out of line," he said. "They were very nonchalant, as if I were questioning a hundred-dollar charge."

IRS gives wrong advice—but makes you pay

A recent study by the Treasury Department found that IRS employees gave incorrect answers in response to taxpayers' questions 47% of the time. The real problem: If you follow their wrong advice, you're still liable for the money—plus penalties.

IRS tries to dig up dead taxpayer's body

In 1990, after a Nebraska man indicted for allegedly offering an IRS agent a bribe had died, the IRS decided it wanted to make sure. It seemed the dead man may have owed upward of $156,000 in back taxes. After grilling the daughter and examining the death certificate, they still wanted to dig up the body and really make *sure*. An attorney for the dead taxpayer's estate noted that under Nebraska law the only legal cause for exhumation was for dissection of the body to find out cause of death. "I've heard the IRS does that to people while they're still alive," he said, "but not when they're dead."

In nuclear attacks against America, IRS plans to help— by collecting taxes from surviving victims

According to the Internal Revenue Service Handbook, under "Emergency Relocation Planning and Operations," in the event of a "national emergency resulting from enemy attack, the essential functions of the Service will be as follows: (1) assessing, collecting, and recording taxes. . . . "

IRS is rude to customers

According to Pete Du Pont of the National Center for Policy Analysis, a 2001 report by the Treasury Department discovered plain old rudeness at the IRS. Treasury agents disguised as humble taxpayers were:

- left waiting for 90 minutes—then given a stack of papers and told to do their own homework
- told that the IRS tax-help office wasn't answering any more questions that day—at 11:00 in the morning
- given wrong answers in well over 50% of the cases (61 wrong answers out of 90)

IRS harasses worker by giving superrefunds then threatening her

The IRS can't stop giving a Missouri supermarket worker mega-refunds—and then threatening her. In 2000, Diana

CREDIT WHERE CREDIT IS DUE . . .

When it comes to monumental rudeness, the IRS has nothing on our British cousins, whose Inland Revenue last year sent a woman a letter telling her: "F*** U W****R". The obscene note was sent in an official brown envelope on official "With Compliments" note paper, according to the West Midlands *Express & Star.* Inland Revenue said this was "not typical of the Inland Revenue's commitment to customer service."

Doss wrongly received a check from the IRS for $188,368.44. She contacted the IRS and was told to write "VOID" on the check and return it. She did. A year later, she got another check from the IRS—for $188,368.44. After she called the IRS, the IRS warned her not to cash the check, or else she would face severe penalties. Doss now has a fear of big checks in the mail. "When I open the mail, I'm just devastated. It's a lot of stress on me."

The Most Fascinating Tax Write-offs

We all pay taxes; and we suspect that we all dislike paying taxes.

But there are those Americans who don't simply pay taxes—they exercise incredible ingenuity and creativity in preparing their tax returns. Unfortunately, often these examples of breathtaking creativity are disallowed by the IRS, which apparently does not believe in rewarding imagination.

What Was Deducted	Type of Deduction	Explanation
breast enlargement	business expense	waitress said she got bigger tips since she got bigger breasts

Action Taken: Accountant talked her out of it

What Was Deducted	Type of Deduction	Explanation
breast enlargement	medical expense	claimed by Detroit stripper Chesty Morgan

Action Taken: Tax-court judge disallowed this deduction . . . but did allow her to write it off as an unreimbursed business expense, which wound up saving her more money

What Was Deducted	Type of Deduction	Explanation
mink coat	business expense	woman said she performed better at work when she looked her best

Action Taken: Not allowed by IRS

What Was Deducted	Type of Deduction	Explanation
dentures that fell into toilet at work	business expense	man said they were work-related loss

Action Taken: Man's accountant talked him out of it (after laughing)

What Was Deducted	Type of Deduction	Explanation
child	dependent deduction	man *did* have child but had neglected to file for the child's Social Security number, which is necessary for deduction

Action Taken: Denied by IRS—after man sent in dirty diapers as proof that he actually did have a child. He fought the case in court . . . and lost.

What Was Deducted	Type of Deduction	Explanation
a dog named Red	dependent deduction	filed by Wyoming disc jockey

What Was Deducted	Type of Deduction	Explanation

Action Taken: Allowed by IRS for several years. After coming clean to his accountant—who then told him to tell the IRS the truth—the DJ took a more creative way out . . . and listed Red as "deceased" on his next tax return. (He never was penalized.)

What Was Deducted	Type of Deduction	Explanation
cost for lobbying voters to get approval to carry a 10-pound wooden ventriloquist's dummy while on patrol	business deduction	claimed by a San Francisco police officer who had patrolled with the dummy but had been told to stop because it made the department look foolish. He spent nearly $11,500 campaigning directly to the public—which voted that the dummy stay

Action Taken: IRS disallowed this and charged him with $3,500 in back taxes

What Was Deducted	Type of Deduction	Explanation
dog food	business expense	claimed by a traveling consultant since his dog traveled with him

Action Taken: Not allowed by IRS

What Was Deducted	Type of Deduction	Explanation
dead wife's ashes	casualty loss	claimed by a tax planner who felt that, since the funeral home lost his wife's ashes, he was entitled to write off the loss

Action Taken: Not allowed by IRS

What Was Deducted	Type of Deduction	Explanation
fee paid to a "business consultant" (who happened to be an arsonist)	business expense	claimed by a Raleigh, North Carolina, furniture-store owner whose business was destroyed by fire

Action Taken: He had received $500,000 in insurance money and paid taxes on that. But he also deducted a $10,000 fee paid to a consultant . . . who was the arsonist he hired to burn down his failing business. Both the "consultant" and the store owner were prosecuted

The Rich and Their Charitable Tax Write-offs

What to do when you make a great deal of money and you need to be sure you get every write-off possible? You get a sharp accountant who can tell you exactly what to claim and how, of course.

Herewith a few prime examples:

How to Save Money on Your Taxes, Dick Cheney-Style

Need a good write-off? Follow the lead of Vice President Dick Cheney and assign a monetary value to time you give to a charitable organization. On his tax return, Cheney did just this for his (theoretically) pro bono speeches. In other words, when he was giving a speech and not accepting any pay for it, he *kinda* was. . . . He was getting a *tax deduction*! He valued those lectures at $232,320 and added that amount into his charitable-donations deduction.

TRUTH IS STRANGER THAN FICTION DEPARTMENT

In a particularly odd move—and one we seriously doubt will attract many takers—both Arkansas and Virginia passed legislation in 2002 allowing citizens to *volunteer* to pay more taxes. One state senator who pushed for the law explained that this innovative idea would let citizens show their support for their government. The money would go into a general fund . . . and legislators would ultimately decide just how to spend the money.

How to Save Money on Your Taxes, Bill Clinton-Style

Remember the old adage "A penny saved is a penny earned," regardless of how much money you make. Thus, remember to itemize everything you can and do not overlook any possible write-off—even the most mundane or easily forgotten. For example, underwear. On Clinton's 1986 tax return, when he was governor of Arkansas, listed under charitable contributions (as merchandise donated) was the following: "3 pr. underwear—$6."

How to Save Money on Your Taxes, Donald Trump-Style

Why donate when you can just keep the cash? This seems to be the credo of Trump, whose level of charitable contributions isn't quite in line with his wealth—at least according to what the Donald J. Trump Foundation donates. According to www.thesmokinggun.com, said foundation seems a tad tightfisted. Case in point: Trump (who is said to be worth roughly $1.6 billion) had his foundation shell out $212,403 in donations in 1998 . . . or 0.00013% of his money. This would be the same as someone earning

$60,000 a year donating $7.80. In 1999, he did even worse: $157,950 in donations (0.0001%)—or, for a person making $60,000, a whopping $6.00.

Our Tax Dollars at Work

Perhaps you wonder just what your tax money goes to. Wonder no longer.

Investigating stolen sandwiches

Federal authorities were called to the airport in Des Moines, Iowa, in 2003 after a federal security officer reported her peanut-butter sandwich was missing from the lunchroom. Apparently, only 16 federal security workers had access to the room, which is entered by punching a secret code into a keypad next to the door. "By the letter of the law, it's a theft," said Lieutenant David Huberty of the area police, "but sending a detective out to the airport to interview 16 people over a missing sandwich would be, I think, inappropriate use of resources."

Developing digital bugle inserts to allow for flawless versions of "Taps"

In late 2002, the Pentagon introduced a portable digital musical insert for a bugle, enabling "Taps" to be played by anyone—musicians and nonmusicians alike, ensuring that mourners at funerals will hear a perfect version of "Taps."

Spending more than $800,000 to give vital feng shui lessons to the poor

The Department of Housing and Urban Development under the Clinton administration ran a New Age wellness program for poor public-housing tenants that included the ancient Asian practice of feng shui, which is based on the premise of not disturbing the bones of dragons buried under the earth. Lucky tenants were taught, according to the *New York Post*, "to burn incense, carry lucky gemstones, and wear feel-good colors like apricot to reduce stress."

The Top Nine Stupidest Tax-Related Things Ever Said

9. Can you lower my taxes, please? I was really unhappy with my tax bracket. I work hard, and I want to keep my earnings.

   —U.S. Open champion Venus Williams, in a telephone conversation with President Bill Clinton

8. For purposes of paragraph (3), an organization described in paragraph (2) shall be deemed to include an organization described in section 501(c)(4), (5) or (6) which would be described in paragraph (2) if it were an organization described in section 501(c)(3).

   —section of the Internal Revenue Code

7. Illegal income, such as stolen or embezzled money, must be included in your gross income.

   —helpful information posted on the official Internal Revenue Service website

6. You will find it a distinct help . . . if you know and look as if you know what you are doing.

   —IRS training manual for tax auditors

5. Passive activity income *does not* include the following: Income for an activity that is not a passive activity.

   —IRS Instructions for Form 8582, Passive Activity Loss Limitations

4. Bribes and kickbacks to governmental officials are deductible unless the individual has been convicted of making the bribe or has entered a plea of not guilty or nolo contendere.

   —item in the IRS official taxpayers' guide

3. Many taxpayers will be inconvenienced by the hostilities [of thermonuclear war] and will have to be excused from paying the normal rate of interest on their debts.

   —IRS study

2. I want to find out who this FICA guy is and how come he's taking so much of my money.

   —Nick Kypreos, then New York Rangers forward, explaining what he planned to do during his Stanley Cup–winning team's visit to the White House

1. Like, a lot of us are making a lot of money now, and so we're paying a lot of taxes, you know. Is there, like, a way I can just write on the memo line of my check what I want my taxes to go for, like for school?

   —actress Justine Bateman at a lecture given by Senator John Kerry (D-Massachusetts)

Stupid Business in the U.S.A.

The business of America is business. Sometimes we do it right. Sometimes we do it wrong. And sometimes we do it stupidly. . . .

How to Lose Your Job

The first element in any business is its employees. American employees get job evaluations; they are tested, probed, and otherwise scrutinized. Books, seminars, websites, and articles focus on the business of getting and holding a job. As there's so much written on this topic, we feel it incumbent on us to explain how to do something even harder: lose a job. Herewith, some very innovative job-losing techniques:

Helpful hint #1: Urinate on your customer's prize collection

A Philadelphia Gas Works (PGW) employee was dispatched to a customer's home to reestablish his gas service. In the basement, he came upon the customer's collection of sports cards—all 3,500 of them arranged neatly. Then, for reasons unknown, he urinated on them. The homeowner had a surveillance camera set up and claimed he caught the incident on tape. He also claimed, in the lawsuit he brought against PGW, that the worker not only urinated but also defecated on the cards. PGW settled the lawsuit for $4,500 and fired the worker.

Helpful hint #2: Hand out brownies baked with laxatives to your coworkers

On January 27, 2000, an Ebensburg, Pennsylvania, man made brownies laced with laxatives as revenge against coworkers who kept eating his bag lunches. Not only did he get fired, he also was denied unemployment compensation, as the court ruled he was guilty of willful misconduct and "evil design." In addition, one of the coworkers who ate the brownies filed a lawsuit against him, seeking unspecified damages for pain and embarrassment.

Helpful hint #3: Show a photo of a nude boy in the middle of your PowerPoint slide show

A Fort Worth, Texas, man was fired after, having finished a PowerPoint presentation, he opened another document on his laptop, which turned out to be a photograph of a nude boy. The man claimed that a computer virus caused it, but police later found more child porn on computer disks taken from him, as well as 65 pages of printed child porn in his desk. He was fired and arrested for possessing and promoting child pornography.

Helpful hint #4: Write a fake news script (and send it to all network affiliates) with the headline "Al Gore arrested today for killing a child with his teeth"

A freelancer at ABC News's Southwest Regional Bureau in Dallas, Texas, wrote a fake script that supposedly originated at his station, WFAA, then accidently sent it to the other ABC network affiliate stations. He was fired.

Helpful hint #5: If you're a teacher, send "humorous" Valentine's Day cards to your students that contain the inscription: "Die, die, die"

A Catholic high school teacher in Phoenix gave a 17-year-old boy in his class a Valentine's Day card that said, "I hate you, I wish you would die; Happy V Day, Die, Die, Die." According to the police report, the teacher had given similar cards to other students, many of whom felt it was just a joke. But the one student was "freaked out" and told the authorities. The teacher was placed on administrative leave.

Helpful hint #6: Call your boss and say you're being robbed at gunpoint

In what was supposed to be an April Fool's Day joke, a clothing-store salesperson called her manager at home, saying there was a thief in the store with a gun asking for all the money. The salesperson called back a few minutes later to shout, "April Fool!" but the manager had already called 911—and four police cars showed up at the store. The saleswoman was arrested for "inducing panic"—a charge that could garner her six months in jail and a $1,000 fine. She was also fired.

Helpful hint #7: Walk out to cash a check while you're in the middle of operating on someone

Dr. David Arndt of Massachusetts needed to cash a check and was worried the bank would close before he was done with his work. So he ducked out for about 30 minutes, putting his work on hold. Unfortunately, his work was orthopedic surgery. When he left his workplace—the operating room—he also left a spinal-surgery patient on the operating table under anesthesia . . . with an open incision in his back. The Massachusetts Board of Registration in Medicine pulled his medical license, pending an appeal.

Helpful hint #8: And finally . . . that old standby: choke your boss

Basketball player Latrell Sprewell took matters into his own hands (literally) when angered by his coach, P. J. Carlesimo, he choked him courtside. His defense (given on *60 Minutes*) included the following: "I wasn't choking P.J. I mean, P.J., he could breathe. It's not like he was losing air or anything like that. I mean, it wasn't a choke, I wasn't trying to kill P.J. If you're choking someone, you don't get scratches. You get welts totally around your neck. It's not like I was going to sit there and kill the man. No, I would have stopped, definitely." (Note: Sprewell did not actually lose his job. The team suspended him but had to pay him the $16.3 million owed on his contract.)

Our Warmhearted, Civic-Minded, Friendly Corporations

We all know that making a profit is only incidental; most large corporations are in business to help make the world a better place. Corporations try to help their employees out; they are personally concerned about their customers; they *truly* care about the world around them. Isn't that what their ads say? Here are some examples of our corporate giants at their very best. . . .

Kindly Steve Madden shoe company markets a "charity" shoe honoring 9/11 firefighters—but keeps the money

After resigning as the CEO of his own company (having been indicted on fraud charges), designer Steve Madden came up with a new image-enhancing idea: a flag-themed shoe called the "Bravest" to "raise money for New York City's fallen firefighters." One problem: none of the profits went to anyone but Steve Madden—until reporters began looking into the scheme. After this, the company's new CEO, Jamie Karson, pledged to give a specified percentage to charities. The amount: a measly 10%. Karson justified it by saying, "The most patriotic thing we can do is make money."

Dow Jones subsidiary <u>The Wall Street Journal</u> gets involved with schoolchildren—by threatening to sue their newspaper

The Wall Street Journal's lawyers didn't take the situation lightly: They contacted publishers of *The Small Street Jour-*

nal, citing name-infringement problems. *The Small Street Journal* is published in Bangor, Maine. Containing puzzles, coloring pages, and educational activities and distributed free of charge in the tiny town of Newburgh, Maine, its intended audience is children under 10.

Helpful Wal-Mart finally helps out trapped 73-year-old lady—after turning her down three times

In 2002, a 73-year-old lady outside a Wal-Mart in Geneseo, Illinois, bought a newspaper and found herself trapped when the door of the newspaper rack suddenly closed and caught her coat. Unable to wiggle out, she called a bystander to go inside the Wal-Mart and get help.

A Wal-Mart employee came out—and then explained she couldn't help. There was a "policy" against tampering with the news rack. The woman would have to stay trapped. The Wal-Mart employee then went back inside.

A short while later, the Wal-Mart employee returned—with an idea. She offered to call the newspaper company that *owned* the rack; maybe they could do something—like drive down and release the lady. The trapped woman angrily countered with another, much easier idea: Couldn't Wal-Mart simply lend/give her two quarters and put them in the newspaper rack—and let her simply open the door and free her coat?

The Wal-Mart employee rejected this obvious idea outright. Wal-Mart couldn't give out money to customers!

Finally, the Wal-Mart employee gave in and put two quarters in the machine and the woman was released. A short while later, the woman's daughter visited the store and gave Wal-Mart a donation of $5 for releasing any future senior citizens or others trapped in the newspaper rack. An

⭐

VOMITING DISNEY

On a 2002 voyage of the Disney cruise ship *Magic,* 288 passengers fell sick on account of the stomach-churning Norwalk virus. Disney promptly gave the ship a thorough disinfecting. The good ship *Magic* set sail a week later. The disinfecting must have worked. This time only 60 passengers got sick to their stomachs.

embarrassed Wal-Mart spokesperson apologized for the incident, saying, "This is not how we do business."

Caring Disney won't let employees wear their own underwear

Disney employees who wear the costumes of Mickey Mouse and others were until recently not allowed to wear their own underwear—instead, they had to wear dirty Disney underwear. The problem was that regular underwear tended to bunch and gather and show under the costumes; so Disney decided to issue employees official, specially designed Mickey costume–friendly underwear instead. Fine. But frugal Disney required people to turn in their special underwear every night—and get another set issued the next day. A different set, worn by someone else. Workers were not happy. Although Disney claimed to be using hot water to clean the underwear that was turned in, employees said the underwear was sometimes stained or smelly. Several reported getting pubic lice and scabies from the underwear. In the words of one employee, "I don't want to share my tights, and I don't want to share my underwear!"

Safety-conscious Microsoft puts decals on road signs

In a clever method of promoting its MSN 8 online service, Microsoft hired people to place hundreds of butterfly-shaped decals throughout Manhattan. They wound up on traffic signals as well as sidewalks. The company eventually apologized and removed the stickers . . . after the city threatened to fine them $50 per decal. (Microsoft did end up paying a fine—of only $50, period.)

Responsible corporate citizen Samuel Adams promotes sex in public places

In August 2003, Jim Koch, chairman of the board of the company that makes Samuel Adams beer, appeared on a New York City radio program to promote its "Sex for Sam" competition, which encouraged couples to have sex in public places throughout the city. One couple decided to have sex in Manhattan's St. Patrick's Cathedral—and were aired live, blow-by-blow (no pun intended, and that's not apparently what was happening anyway), prompting outraged phone calls and the fury of churchgoers. After all the angry complaints, the civic-minded Koch canceled the competition.

Patriotic Verizon helps small towns with post-9/11 security–by charging them a high price

In the late winter of 2003, the police department in Mahwah, New Jersey, asked their phone company, Verizon, for a list of unpublished numbers to plug into their "reverse 911" system, which calls residences in case of emergency. This is a new routine in today's tenser times. Verizon was happy to comply—for upward of $5,000. With rates like this, Verizon, which keeps the database for all unlisted numbers in New Jersey, stands to make millions. Verizon was unfazed by towns asking for something of a patriotic discount. Said the Mahwah police chief, Verizon "told me there was no room for discussion. . . . They were adamant about the price." According to him, "This is revenue-generating for them; they don't seem worried about public safety." After the local powerhouse Bergen *Record* newspaper called Verizon, the company suddenly said it was "reevaluating" things. Stay tuned.

Charitable Apple Computer dumps computers in landfill instead of donating them

In the early 1990s, after Apple's Lisa computer proved to be a flop, the company buried 2,700 unsold ones in a Utah landfill. Why didn't they donate them to one of the many schools clamoring for new computers? By dumping them, they got a better tax write-off.

Civic-minded IBM spray paints Chicago with graffiti

They were all over sidewalks on Chicago's North Side in 2001—a trail of black, spray-painted stencils of a peace symbol, a heart, and a smiling penguin. The city eventually discovered the culprit—not some delinquent kid but corporate giant IBM, which was using the stencils as part of its "Peace, Love, and Linux" advertising campaign. Chicago officials were not amused—saying that they would charge the company $67 for cleanup.

When Goliath Fights David . . . with an Uzi

Companies have the right, of course, to protect their brand names, their intellectual property, and so forth. This is the case, theoretically, because a company doesn't want the public to be confused or otherwise scammed, shall we say, into confusing their product or work with that of an imitator. But a review of some particularly engaging cease-and-desist cases leads one to believe that it is highly unlikely that the public would be at all confused . . . and that perhaps the corporations in question are a tad too concerned. (Perhaps "anal" is a better choice of a word.)

Goliath: AOL Time Warner
David: founder of *Niggertainment Monthly*

Yes, you're thinking exactly what we're thinking: *Niggertainment Monthly* sounds almost exactly like *Entertainment Weekly,* and you might wind up buying the wrong magazine. Well, that's what AOL Time Warner apparently thought when they filed suit against the small Yonkers hip-hop magazine. The founder had to pull 700,000 copies of the magazine from newsstands when the suit was filed, pending resolution.

Goliath: Paramount Studios (as owners of *Star Trek*)
David: Dallas mayor Ron Kirk

Kirk used the theme music of the television show *Star Trek* and allusions to the show in a campaign ad: "Four years ago, we chose Ron Kirk captain of the Dallas Enterprise." While voters presumably did not think that Kirk was Captain James Tiberius Kirk, nor even William Shatner—or that Dallas was similar to the USS *Enterprise*—Paramount seemed very worried by the possibility. They sent Kirk a cease-and-desist letter. The ad was pulled.

Goliath: fashion company Tommy Hilfiger

David: manufacturers of Timmy Holedigger canine perfume

A small company made a fragrance for dogs called Timmy Holedigger. While Tommy Hilfiger has no line for pets (as yet), the company felt that the scent was a threat to its trademark and that consumers might get confused. A federal judge believed no such confusion was likely and rejected the lawsuit. (The makers of Timmy Holedigger also put out another canine fragrance named Poochi, but neither Gucci nor Pucci have filed suit.)

Goliath: Prema Toy Company (trademark owners of Gumby and Gumby's pal Pokey the horse, among others)

David: 12-year-old Chris Van Allen, owner of the domain name pokey.org

Van Allen used his nickname, Pokey, for a website, little suspecting that he had created a (Claymation) monster. Prema Toy Company, owner of the names "Gumby" and "Pokey," went after the kid for daring to use his own nickname (and, of course, not checking in with trademark lawyers prior to registering the domain name). Turn over the trade name or face a lawsuit, it said. Fortunately, the case caught the attention of the media; Gumby creator Art Clokey interceded on Van Allen's behalf and, worried even more about the bad publicity, Prema dropped its demand.

Goliath: Archie Comics

David: proud father David Sams, who set up a website, www.veronica.org, named after his 2-year-old daughter

In Archie Comics, Veronica is the dark-haired rich girl who competes with blond Betty for Archie's affections. On the web, Veronica was a toddler whose proud father had

**COMING CLEAN:
GREAT MOMENTS IN BUSINESS LAWSUITS**

The following exchange occurred during a Florida lawsuit against tobacco manufacturer Philip Morris in 1996:

Florida prosecutor: "Would Philip Morris agree that a single American citizen who smokes their products for thirty or more years, a single one, has ever died of a disease caused in part by smoking?"

Philip Morris chairman Geoffrey Bible: "I think there's a fair chance that one would have, might have."

bought the domain name www.veronica.org to set up a site on which he posted photos of her. Well, baby Veronica happens to have a trademarked name, said Archie Comics, which demanded Sams turn over the domain name. They finally dropped their case, explaining that their only goal was to protect children from stumbling upon an "inappropriate site."

Stupid Advertising, Marketing, and Products in the U.S.A.

Whether you're a consumer, a product developer, or an advertising exec, the U.S. is a paradise. But sometimes that paradise is more like a bit of hell. . . . Are we making sense here?

Really Bad American Products

The United States is truly the land of innovation—not only the land where the lightbulb was invented but, more important, the land where the lightbulb was first packaged and sold. Every year, Americans develop and market more new products than do any other people on earth. Some of these products are wonderful, bold new ideas that excite the public and make billions for the corporations selling them. Others, however, are not.

So let us give a hand to good ol' American ingenuity when it comes to product development . . . and the ever-hopeful thought that perhaps *this* is something the public will have to have. Among the more dubious products introduced in the U.S.A.:

Premier and Eclipse (RJR Nabisco)

The great idea: a smokeless cigarette that delivers taste, not health problems

The problem: "It tastes like shit!"

These words came from the company's own CEO. Premier was quickly withdrawn, company executives rightly fearing that an excrement-flavored cigarette might not attract many buyers. One hundred million dollars later, the company produced Eclipse, which quickly lived up to its name. The problem: Nonsmokers liked the idea of a smokeless cigarette but smokers didn't; they wanted to smoke, literally. And guess what? Nonsmokers don't buy cigarettes. A bomb.

Fresh and Lite low-fat frozen Chinese food (La Choy)

The great idea: convenient low-fat frozen entrées—just pop in the microwave and serve!

The problem: the name "Fresh and Lite," for one

"It sounded more like a feminine hygiene product," said one person who worked on the ad campaign. Besides, it wasn't fresh, it was frozen. Then there were the frozen egg rolls . . . designed to complement the fresh and light meals. They were too big: Put them in the microwave, and out came a soggy mess; put them in the oven, and it took 30 long minutes. Soggy, sounds like a feminine hygiene product, not fresh, hard to cook. Not a success.

Microsoft Bob (Microsoft)

The great idea: a cute, "fun" user-interface shell program designed to help you through all of your software problems!

The problem: sickeningly cutesy

People really hated Microsoft Bob, a cute little cartoon guy with glasses who was the "star" of the program and helped you out with your software problems. The first product Bill Gates launched personally, he said it was going to be big. Real Big. Bob turned your screen into a cute little house; all you had to do was click on the appropriate image and Bob would do the rest—like get the application you needed up and running. Want to send some e-mail? Click onto the cute little letter on Bob's cute desk and presto: Just write a letter. Bob had a bunch of cute little friends to help—like Rover, a cute computer doggie, and Scuzz, the cute little scuzzy mouse. But they all died a quick death—people just couldn't stand them. Gates didn't get the message: A short time later, he came out with a brand *new* set of Office Assistants in Office 97. Not Bob, but Mr. Paper Clip, cute Clippy the dancing paper clip, another nauseatingly annoying Microsoft helper. And now that that's all history, many computer experts are saying that Microsoft Bob was just ahead of its time. . . . Yet another sickening Microsoft character is now in the works.

Wine and Dine Dinner (Heublin)

The great idea: an upscale packaged meal with an entrée and a fun little bottle of wine for today's modern, on-the-move couples who want instant gourmet

The problem: undrinkable wine

The "fun little bottle of wine" was filled with cooking wine, with salt and spices thrown in. You were supposed to add it to the meal and heat. Most customers didn't bother reading the directions and quaffed the wine, which tasted like salty swill. Even worse, without the wine flavoring, the dinner tasted like bland mush.

Funky Fries (Heinz)

The great idea: French fries in funky new flavors and colors—blue, chocolate, and cinnamon!

The problem: a little *too* funky

As one expert put it, "Who in the world would want to eat blue or chocolate potatoes anyway?" Apparently very few people: In 2003, after only one year, Heinz announced they were pulling the fries off the shelves.

Napa Natural—"The world's first natural soft drink" (Adams Natural Beverage company)

The great idea: a soft drink with natural fruit juice to appeal to the fancy-bottled-water set—with 67% fruit juice and no preservatives, all natural, all delicious

The problem: exploded . . . literally

At first, all went well. In 1984, the first year the drink was introduced, it broke sales records. Then store owners noticed that cans of Napa Natural were beginning to bulge ominously; and then . . . cans began exploding on the shelves. The manufacturers didn't realize that fruit juice without preservatives tends to ferment . . . and lets off gas, which blows up the product. With so much fruit juice in the cans, fermentation happened quickly and violently. The manufacturer eventually reduced the fruit-juice content to 51%, then to 30%, but by that time sales had collapsed; stores were scared to reorder a product that literally exploded off their shelves.

The XFL (NBC and the WWF)

The idea: "smash-mouth" football, no-holds-barred down-and-dirty games in a new league with fewer rules, more violence, camera close-ups in the huddle, and sexier cheerleaders. NBC and the World Wrestling Federation invested $100 million; corporate flacks and magazine writers hyped it all up. They loved it before they saw it. This was going to be big; watch out, NFL!

The problem: NFL laughed all the way to the bank

The football games were terrible. No one had thought about that. Sloppy, dull games. The players, for the most part, weren't that good; it wasn't their fault: They were new and didn't act as a team. TV coverage was laughably bad. Touted as a "new" form of coverage, cameras zoomed in and out of huddles (and especially in and out of close-ups of cheerleaders' bouncing breasts); with all that zooming and bouncing, viewers tended to forget what was happening on the field. Announcers like Jesse Ventura were predictably terrible; at one point, Ventura wasted precious minutes of play time on a diatribe against XFL critics ("They probably never even strapped on a helmet"—yeah, so what, does that mean you can't talk about football if you never played it, Jesse?), almost missing a play. If even hired hacks like Ventura forgot to care about what was happening on the field, who else would remember? After a great start with viewers, in a few short months no one—*no one*—was watching. The 17th game (between the Birmingham Thunderbolts and the Las Vegas Outlaws) achieved one dubious record: With a 1.6 Nielsen rating, it was the lowest rating *ever* for any prime-time network show.

A-Tox

The great idea: BOTOX for cheapskates. No doctor, no injections, and you can buy it over the counter. "Serious Skin Care A-Tox Facial Firming Wrinkle Smoothing Serum"—$29.95 for half an ounce. The ad said you would "see a new youthfulness you may not have seen in years"

The problem: what you really see are chemical burns and dry, flaky skin

The main ingredient in A-Tox was sodium silicate, a highly alkaline and irritating antiseptic mineral. According to the *American Journal of Contact Dermatitis,* when applied to the skin the mineral causes the skin to constrict, pulling wrinkles flat—but the effect is temporary . . . very temporary. It lasts about as long as you can keep your face expressionless. Worse, continued use could give you contact dermatitis.

Stupidest Ad-Campaign Characters

For every Energizer Bunny or Campbell's Soup Kid, there is an ad-campaign character that doesn't quite have the *je ne sais quoi* to capture the public's attention . . . or, in certain cases, can capture attention but for the wrong reasons. Among them:

"Healthy Penis": a smiling flesh-colored penis (complete with testicles) appearing in person, in ads, in posters, on brochures, and as a squeezable stress grip

Healthy Penis is part of a "whimsical" (to use its sponsors' term) ad campaign funded in 2002 by the city of San Francisco (i.e., taxpayers) to help fight syphilis. The slogan:

SOME *MORE* STUPID PRODUCTS YOU PROBABLY WOULD NEVER BUY

- **Snif-T-Panties:** scented women's underwear in fragrances including pizza, banana, popcorn, and whiskey

- **Hop n' Gator:** refreshing lemon-lime–flavored beer

- **Earring Magic Ken:** Barbie's "partner" dressed in black pants, purple faux leather vest, lavender mesh T-shirt, and frosted hair, wearing an earring. (The product didn't sell well to the target audience but became a cult hit with gay men.)

- **Nothing Box:** a box with eight lights that did nothing but blink. Sold by gadget company Hammacher Schlemmer in 1963, the catalog copy included the following sure-fire sales pitch: "It will keep winking its eight eyes in no recognizable pattern and for no apparent reason for nearly a year. Then it's as dead as a mackerel, and you can't get it fixed." It wasn't a complete dud—buyers included President Dwight Eisenhower and the Beatles

- **butt sketches:** portraits of one's posterior painted by Dallas artist Krandel Lee Newton or one of his assistants for $55 and up

- **used Dallas Cowboys socks, pants, shoes, gloves, or jerseys:** as sold on the Dallas Cowboys website, ranging in price from $19.99 to $699.99 and guaranteed to have been worn by an actual Dallas Cowboys player

- **Sound Bites:** lollipops put out by toy company Hasbro that produced "voices in your head" as music and sounds vibrated through the teeth and jaws to the inner ear

- **snap-on hair:** For men who are folliclely challenged, a New York doctor, Anthony Pignataro, invented a toupee that snaps into metal plugs that are surgically implanted in the head. While the invention got a decent amount of press initially, it still hasn't grown on the public

- **Grenade shampoo:** introduced in 1992 and discontinued shortly thereafter, it was sold in a bottle that looked like a grenade and boasted the ad copy: "Pull the pin, you'll know it's real!"
- **All Weather Windshield Wash:** a product that sounds good until you read the fine print, where you learn: All Weather Windshield Wash is for "use in temperatures above 32 degrees F. (May freeze in temperatures below 32 degrees F.)"

"Making Every Penis a Healthy Penis." Healthy Penis is often accompanied by a syphilis sore—a red snarling blob. Healthy Penis sees a doctor (an African-American penis wearing a white coat), lifts weights, and goes to the bathhouse, among other things. For those who may be curious, there is no corresponding Healthy Vagina character— perhaps because the campaign is aimed at the gay male population. See www.healthypenis2003.org.

"Phil the Syphilis Sore": a red snarling blob—the counterpoint to the happy Healthy Penis

The city of Los Angeles rejected the Healthy Penis campaign, as health officials felt it too racy, demeaning to the gay community, and potentially offensive to others. Said the chief of public health operations, many feared that "the penis actually sort of objectified gay men as penises, which was a concern." In place, they have instituted the ostensibly less racy Phil the Syphilis Sore campaign—costing taxpayers $394,000. (Phil wears silver shoes and an earring, but no one felt this might be a bit of stereotyping.) The campaign includes ads, a Phil stress gripper, and two life-size Phil mascots that make appearances through the city. Interestingly, the cartoons are the same as those in Healthy Penis, but the part played by Healthy Penis in San Francisco is simply a man in a T-shirt, jeans, and a goatee.

"Herb the Nerd": an archetypal nerd—complete with thick glasses, white socks, and flood pants

Herb headlined a $40 million campaign designed in 1985 by agency J. Walter Thompson for Burger King . . . and became synonymous with failure. Herb was a character who, shockingly, had never eaten at Burger King. The campaign featured mock interviews with Herb's family and friends and asked you to "spot Herb" in your neighborhood Burger King. No one cared much about Herb, other than comedians and the advertising press, which lampooned it. This was one of J. Walter Thompson's biggest busts—and one of the decade's biggest ad failures.

"Jesus Christ": yes, *that* Jesus Christ, who appeared in not one but *two* ad campaigns in the recent past

Most recently, in April 2003, Jesus was seen on a billboard (courtesy People for the Ethical Treatment of Animals) with the tagline "Jesus was the Prince of Peas." Even better, this Jesus had a tasteful (and tasty) orange slice as a halo. The campaign was launched to coincide with both Passover and Easter in an attempt to steer people away from meat. Not surprisingly, people found the campaign distasteful (perhaps the orange slice was the straw that broke the camel's back?) and inaccurate (as one rabbi pointed out, slaughtering lambs was customary among Jews of that period). Jesus also was the headliner in a 2002 campaign against SUVs that posited the pressing question: "What would Jesus drive?" (No one was quite sure, although there were those who felt Jesus would probably choose an electric

POSSIBLY THE STUPIDEST AD CAMPAIGN EVER WRITTEN

Award-winning adman Stan Freberg wrote the following—a full-page newspaper ad for small Pacific Airlines. Two months after the campaign started, the airline went bankrupt. Perhaps the ad was involved.

Hey there! You with the sweat in your palms. It's about time an airline faced up to something. Most people are scared witless of flying. Deep down inside, every time that big plane lifts off that runway, you wonder if this is it, right? You want to know something, fella? So does the pilot, deep down inside.

car.") In yet another recent ad, a man standing in line for communion holds a bowl of onion dip made from Lipton Soup, apparently seeking to improve the taste of communion bread, the body of Christ. Not surprisingly, this ad was greeted with protests and was withdrawn.

Seven Stupid Ways to Promote Goods or Services

Promotions are *supposed* to get you clients or customers. Sometimes, though, things don't quite work out the way the promotion/publicity geniuses planned.

1. Send prospective clients (faux) hand grenades

Los Angeles business-litigation firm Quinn Emanuel sent out 600 packages containing fake hand grenades—actually paperweights—to prospective clients. "Business is war" was their catchy slogan. One partner explained that their "marketing consultant told us this is Silicon Valley, they're youthful, kind of aggressive, edgy; this is an effective promotion to do." It was so effective that the Santa Clara bomb squad was called in to several mail locations. The campaign was, to put it aptly, a bomb . . . so it was scrapped. "I guess their ad guy is going to be selling refrigerators in Guam," said a bomb-squad member.

2. Send (fake) ransom notes to CEOs

New York ad agency Berenter, Greenhouse & Webster (which specialized in the toy market) came up with a hot way to get more business: Send ransom notes to the CEOs of companies they'd like to represent, along with a small gift. Many recipients realized it was a promotion. But the people at William Wrigley worried that perhaps the CEO's children were being stalked by a kidnapper. They called in the FBI, which launched an investigation (including determining who might have written the note—an educated woman, they concluded). After 10 days, the FBI deduced that it was a promotional gimmick and didn't prosecute but did warn the ad agency.

3. Offer a case of Snapple to the family of the 1,000th person to commit suicide by jumping off the Golden Gate Bridge

This was supposed to be a humorous, tongue-in-cheek promotion offered by disc jockeys at a San Francisco radio station. But some listeners did not find this as amusing as the radio personalities did.

4. Cross-promote McRib sandwiches and Animal Kingdom theme park

A cross-promotion devised by Disney (owners of Animal Kingdom) and McDonald's (makers of the McRib) was met with criticism by consumers and marketing pundits alike. A McDonald's spokesman explained, however, that the charge that the matchup seemed a tad incongruous was incorrect: "Animal Kingdom is very much a wild experience and the McRib is a wild taste that allows customers to experience the fun and magic of the Animal Kingdom without going to Orlando."

5. Offer special discounts to clergymen—at a sex store that happens to be near a Baptist church

Pure Pleasure, an adult-entertainment store in Stewartville, Minnesota, came up with a clever promotional idea: offer clergy discount and promote it on the double-sided outdoor sign that is visible by those going to and from the nearby Baptist church. Those approaching the church read: "And God said go out into the world and have great sex. God's gift to women. Amen and amen." Those leaving: "No need to mail order. Gay videos in stock. Clergy discount. Have good sex. Hallelujah!" The sign has incurred the wrath of churchgoers and clergy, but no action has been taken.

6. Bring a life-size Timothy McVeigh dummy to a radio-show promotion so guests can "execute" him

KFI (Los Angeles) talk-show hosts Tim Kelly and Nell Saavedra thought this was a brilliant concept for their live on-air party: bring the McVeigh dummy to a Long Beach bar, then let patrons stick him with toy syringes. Oddly enough, the bar owner gave the concept a thumbs-down and didn't allow it.

7. Encourage college students to drink beer instead of milk

PETA (People for the Ethical Treatment of Animals) thinks milk is cruel to cows and bad for our bodies; and so, in 1999, they launched a campaign on college campuses suggesting that students switch to beer instead. They even passed out little PETA keychains that doubled as bottle openers. If PETA wanted massive publicity they got it: *USA Today* featured the president of Mothers Against Drunk Driving railing against the group, calling alcohol the "number 1 drug problem"; PETA's website and phone lines were deluged with calls from angry parents. PETA was forced to end the campaign early.

And . . . the promotion that is in the worst possible taste whatsoever:

In its campaign to get a free stadium from the government, the Minnesota Twins baseball team ran a TV ad warning, "If the Twins leave Minnesota, an eight-year old boy from Willmar [Minn.] undergoing chemotherapy will never get a visit from [Twins player] Marty Cordova." It turns out that the eight-year-old was from out of state and already dead. Worse yet, the Twins got the footage of the dying boy under false pretenses, having promised to use it to promote the team's community activism.

NOT IN THE TRADITION OF EDWARD R. MURROW

CNN ran a promotion for news anchor Paula Zahn, with voice-overs announcing her as "just a little bit sexy"; as the words "provocative" and "sexy" flashed across the screen, a close-up appeared—of Paula Zahn's lips. Zahn complained, and the ad campaign was pulled.

Appallingly Bad Taste Department

Bad taste is not wholly American, but we Americans certainly have a knack for it . . . especially when there's money to be made from it. Who needs good taste when there's a profit involved? Or so, we assume, thought those responsible for the following. . . .

"Shock and Awe" trademark applications

Amid the Iraq war and media coverage of the "shock and awe" bombing campaign, ever-alert businesses rushed to trademark the phrase for a wide range of products—the day after the war started. Among them: Sony (which had planned to use the name for a new combat video game but dropped the application after getting flack from consumers), a Texas pesticide company, an Ohio fireworks firm, a California T-shirt designer, and a New York maker of beer mugs and decorative plates. In addition, a Mansfield, Texas, man hoped to control the term for a number of uses, including "inflatable bath toys," "aftermarket automobile products," "alcoholic beverages," "smoking jackets," and "television programming."

TRUTH IN ADVERTISING: WHAT AD GROUPS REALLY THINK ABOUT PROMOTIONS

Advertising and Promotion. Understanding the difference between persuasion and bribery.

—American Association of Advertising Agencies headline for their own promotional ad (it was quickly recalled)

"World Trade Center" trademark application

At 2:40 P.M. on September 11, 2001, Michael Heiden, a New Jersey restauranteur, filed a claim with the U.S. Patent and Trademark Office to trademark the words "World Trade Center." Heiden said that since Disney trademarked "Pearl Harbor" before producing its film of that name, he figured he'd trademark "World Trade Center" first, saying, "if they ever do make a movie, I'd like to get involved."

"Let's Roll" trademark application

At least 12 people or corporations tried to trademark the phrase "Let's roll," used by the hero Todd Beamer before attempting to overpower some of the 9/11 hijackers. Answering objections from the Todd Beamer Foundation, one trademark applicant, Jack Williams, countered, "I don't care what your name is, it's first in, first swim. . . . It's all about good old American capitalism."

"Hot Seat Extreme"—an "interactive electric chair"

This "fun" amusement-park attraction features an electrocution simulator that billows out smoke at Screams, a Halloween-themed park in Waxahachie, Texas.

Thong underwear—with the words "eye candy" or "wink wink" printed on the front—for girls ages 10 and younger

These were sold by Abercrombie & Fitch, which received complaints from angry parents. The company felt that there was no need for concern since "the underwear for young girls was created with the intent to be lighthearted and cute. Any misrepresentation of that is purely in the eye of the beholder."

Asian-themed fake-company T-shirt (sold, again, by Abercrombie & Fitch) with the slogan "Wong Brothers Laundry Service: Two Wongs Can Make It White"

Consumers complained loudly—and the company got bad press—so the shirts were pulled. Said the spokesman, "We thought everyone would love this T-shirt. We are truly and deeply sorry."

Kaboom: The Suicide Bomber Game—an Internet game that awards more points for bystander victims

The site specializes in games based on contemporary events . . . which explains some of the other games, such as "Extreme WTC Jumper," "Sniper's Revenge," and "Pico's School" (introduced after the Columbine shootings). The webmaster for the site defended the games in a *New York Times* article, explaining that people "need to lighten up and realize there are far worse problems in the world than what games people are playing."

State pen turned into an outlet mall

The city manager of Moundsville, West Virginia, and a group of local businessmen hoped to turn the state penitentiary in their town into a mall, after it closed in 1992. As the city manager explained: "I visualize a very successful outlet shopping mall. We would keep some of the cellblocks to attract people and maybe put the electric chair on display."

Vietnam Village—a Florida tourist theme park circa 1976

The theme park reproduced a typical Vietnamese village during the war, complete with 56 Vietnamese refugees playing the parts of villagers. A spokesperson described what would happen when a tour group entered the park: "We'll have a recording broadcast a fire fight, mortars exploding, bullets flying, Vietnamese screaming. . . . There's nothing offensive about it."

Bad PR

The stupidest opening paragraph of a press release ever written:

Imagine waking up to radio reports that said, "Schools and businesses have been closed because of frozen pizza." Sounds ridiculous, but if all the frozen pizza sold in the United States each year was spread across six states, those radio reports could be true.

—opening paragraph of press release from the National Frozen Pizza Institute

Hooray for the Red, Rhomboid, and Yellow

From a speech made by the manager of design and communications for Oscar Mayer:

> Let's take a look at what we're doing. In much the same way as the Founding Fathers of our country sat down to hammer out the Constitution of this great Republic, we sat down with all the key players and worked out our packaging design strategy.
>
> Our "packaging constitution" defines the rules for everyone. Oh, yes, it has its Bill of Rights. It ensures everyone has an opportunity to participate, to freely express their views. . . . Our "Founding Fathers" have reviewed . . . this packaging material very carefully before they put their John Hancocks on the line. . . .
>
> The red rhomboid with white behind the words "Oscar Mayer" on a yellow field has become the visual standard. Red, rhomboid and yellow are to the supermarket what red, white and blue are to our country. . . . God bless our rhomboid.

Great American Lemons

When it comes to bad cars, we Americans should be proud: the U.S. does not come first. Yugoslavia, a nation that is now defunct, produced a car that was defunct the minute it came off the assembly line: the Yugo, arguably the worst car in history. The Fiat-inspired Yugo may have also been partly inspired by Russian technology: Russian cars are almost as bad, although if you kick a Russian car it usually stays together. The French, with some of their finicky Peugeots and difficult Renaults, are a close third. But the U.S. has had its moments, particularly in the wonder years of the 1970s and early 1980s, when a lot of things just weren't going right in what came to be called the Rust Belt. Here, in loosely reverse order, are the All-American duds:

The Edsel (Ford)

A 1950s oldie favorite of bad-car fans, the Edsel really wasn't so bad.

It was just that the front grill looked like a toilet seat. And designing a car grill to look like a toilet seat was not one of the greatest ideas in U.S. automotive history.

Predictably, the Edsel was designed by a committee. Initially, the idea had been to solicit design advice from thousands of Ford customers; this idea was scrapped, and instead the project was assigned to an unwieldy design committee of Ford executives, managers, and engineers, who did what committees do best. They compromised.

And so the Edsel was a grab bag of bad design. Besides its toilet-seat front grill, the Edsel had huge rear tail fins that made it look ungainly and slow, like a fat duck. Making a car look slow and ungainly even though it's not is another idea that's not so great. And yes, the Edsel had an array of other problems, too—steering disasters and cooling-system foul-ups—but the real problem was that design. Add to that all the hype and publicity surrounding the car: Ford laid it on thick and came out with a visual lemon.

The bottom line? Almost no one bought it. Worse, Ford lost $3,000 for each car sold, which is also not a great way to do business. After two years, it was dumped; economists figured that the company could have given away a new Ford Mercury to each Edsel buyer and still saved money. Before the Edsel came out, Ford had commissioned poet Marianne Moore to come up with a name for it. She did: the Utopian Turtletop, which oddly enough somehow fits.

The Gremlin (AMC)

Another car people love to hate; another design disaster.

The Gremlin mechanically wasn't amazingly bad, and if you weren't the type to worry about a rather lengthy time lapse between you pressing the accelerator and the car actually doing something, this could have been the car for you.

The problem was the design. The Gremlin was a bulbous car that looked . . . tumorous; weird; as one customer said, "calling it a pregnant roller skate would be kind." Its interior design was no great shakes either. The rear seating took the idea of "compact" very literally; you had to do contortions to sit in back. One owner claimed Gremlin rear seats kept the chiropractic industry in business during the 1970s; another called it a 2⅔ seater—two seats in front, two ⅓ seats in back.

The Fuego (AMC and Renault)

This brilliant car model came from combining the mechanical genius of the French with the design genius of the American Motor Company. The result was predictable: a weird-looking car that didn't work.

First of all, the Fuego was prone to electrical shorts; or, to be more precise, very frequent electrical shorts. Second, the engine had a tendency to chug or conk out. Such a car does not leap out of showrooms. One thing going for the Fuego: When it worked, it handled well. And the turbo model was really quite sportif. But most customers preferred cars that started without calling AAA.

The Vega (Chevrolet)

The Chevy Vega was a cheap car that didn't cost much for a very good reason: it was a cheaply made car.

One owner said it was made of "compressed rust"; but most people agreed that it was made of metal—originally, that is. It tended to rust so quickly and heavily that people could forget its metallic origins. Gaping holes in the roof or doors were not uncommon. A few things didn't rust: The cylinders in the engine, for example. The Vega was the first GM car to use, among other things, all aluminum cylinders. While they didn't rust, they didn't work very well either. The Vega didn't go all that fast but it consumed an awful lot of oil, the aluminum engine warped, and the car tended to fall apart in accidents, if it didn't collapse from metal fatigue. Not the type of car you'd want to put a prized crash dummy in.

The Caprice (Chevrolet)

Picked by *Forbes* as one of America's worst cars, this wonder had one thing going for it: an excellent (for its time) EPA rating of 22 mpg.

The only problem was staying on the road long enough to get that good mileage.

To say the car had steering problems was an understatement: It took constant attention and a firm hand on the wheel to keep the car from lurching off the road; later models, fitted with V-8 engines, were even worse—you could veer off the road that much faster. Plus, the Caprice had a suspension that sent the impact with every pothole or crack in the road reverberating up through your jawbone. And, as *Forbes* noted, it was one of the more boring-looking cars of the decade.

The Chevette (Chevrolet)

Another car with good mileage, but so what? Nothing else worked.

The Chevette was built in the days of the gas crisis and booming Japanese compact-car sales as sort of a faux Honda or Toyota; but it was really more of a faux car. One design option even had faux wood panels glued to the side. The Chevette wasn't all faux, however: The floors were made of real plywood. Not surprisingly, the Chevette was plagued with major mechanical failures: ignition problems, leaking transmissions. The car shook at moderate speeds, it wouldn't start in cold weather, and it had poor acceleration—this last really wasn't much of a problem because the car couldn't go that fast anyway. Some people swore it was a law-abiding car: It never went above 55. Maybe the best thing about it was that it rusted easily: wait long enough and it would rust away.

The Cimarron (Cadillac)

A very bad car.

A very, very bad car.

All with a high Cadillac price.

In terms of reliability, much worse than average; it has made the *Consumer Reports* list of used cars to avoid every year since 1988. Problems? Uncontrolled acceleration, power-steering defects, plain old bad steering, fuel-system leaks, brake problems, cracked heads, surging or racing motors, leaking rear main oil seals, piston knocks, headlight lamp failures, light flickers—and here's a fun one—the driver's seat suddenly reclines. Imagine that happening while you're driving. Did we mention the uncontrolled-acceleration problem?

The Pacer (AMC)

In the 1970s, AMC decided to utilize the latest in automotive technology and styling to design the "car of the future."

The result: the Pacer, generally considered to be the ugliest car in the world.

Described as a "rolling greenhouse" and "a bulbous fish-bowl," the egg-shaped Pacer did have some design advantages: It had large windows and gave drivers and riders good views of the road. Problem was that people could easily recognize you driving it. Mechanically, it wasn't so bad; however, it had an annoying tendency to rust in certain places—namely, around the wheels, the underbody frame, the bottom of the back fenders, just under the windshield, the area around the windshield wipers (where, if left unchecked, it caused cracks in the windshield itself), under the license plate, the rear door of the station-wagon version, and, last but not least, the gas tank, especially the area between the car body and the tank. The best epitaph for the Pacer comes from a 1996 article in the San Jose *Mercury News:* "In January in Fremont, Calif., a carjacker ... yanked Cecilia Laus, 54, out of her car and drove off, leaving the woman shaken and also bewildered, since the car was a 1976 AMC Pacer."

The Pinto (Ford)

The only car with its own custom bumper sticker: HIT ME AND WE BLOW UP TOGETHER.

Synonymous with "bad car," the onetime bestselling Pinto turned out to have the nasty habit of bursting into flames on impact. With anything. At almost any speed. The problem was that in an accident, the rear end of the car would buckle like an accordion, the tube leading to the gas-tank cap would be ripped away, and gas would immediately begin sloshing around in and around the car. The buckled gas tank would be jammed against the differential housing, and all you needed was a little spark—from a cigarette, scraping metal, or ignition—and. . . . Another nice touch was that Pinto doors had a tendency to jam at impacts over 40 mph. Just the time to be locked inside. The Pinto had one major advantage though: Like the Pacer, it was one of the least stolen cars in America. Even thieves didn't want it.

IF IT'S GREEN, IT'S BLUE

Because consumers tend not to like the color "green" on their cars, car manufacturers play around with the terminology. For example, one Ford car color, "pastel steel blue frost," was actually more green than blue. According to Bonnie Cunningham, design manager for color and trim at Ford, "It's a very blue-green, almost blue, but it would still be classified in our terms as green. When we were selling this color—because we had not had green in the line-up for so long, to get people comfortable with it we did not call it green, we called it blue."

Stupid Entertainment in the U.S.A.

Let's face it—most entertainment in the U.S.A. is stupid. But there is that which goes so far beyond the limits of normal stupidity that it deserves special credit....

Seven of the Worst Hit TV Show Spin-offs*

Television shows are produced to make money, so the equation is easy. If you've got a hit show on your hands and a lot of dedicated viewers out there in TV land, it's easy to envision one or two or even three little spin-offs in addition to your hit, earning you and your people more megabucks. The problem is that spin-offs (loosely defined here to mean shows derived from other shows, based on characters or ideas developed in the original show) are usually very, very bad. Not always. *Frasier* is a spin-off from *Cheers*, and it's done quite well—both critically and financially. On the other hand....

---

*Not the top seven worst; there are so many it's hard to choose.

1. AfterMASH

Spin-off of: M*A*S*H

Lasted: 14 months

Summary: Here's an exciting idea: Take a hit show about a war—with guns, sex, and an antiwar message—and relocate it to a Midwestern suburb! Without all the stars!

The parent show, M*A*S*H, was the 1970s hit about the adventures of people in an Mobile Army Surgical Hospital unit during a faux–Vietnam War. (Technically, it was set in the Korean War, but it looked 99.99% like a 1970s California version of Vietnam.) After the main stars got bored of the idea and wanted to call it quits, but with CBS pushing for a sequel, three minor stars opted for a new show about life after M*A*S*H—afterM*A*S*H, get it? The players from M*A*S*H who opted in were Harry Morgan (who played the commanding officer, Colonel Potter), William Christopher (who played the chaplain, Father Mulcahy), and Jamie Farr (who played the CO's clerk, Corporal Klinger, and whose claim to fame was that he dressed up in woman's clothing). There was also Rosalind Chao as Klinger's Korean wife, Soon-Lee (who had appeared on a few of the last M*A*S*H shows). Missing were the main stars, the main villains, Klinger's women's clothing, and the main conflict: the war. A show about supporting characters now based in a VA hospital in middle America—in River Bend, Missouri, as a matter of fact—sounds *dull. After-MASH* was. It lasted a little over a season and then died in its sleep.

2. The Ropers

Spin-off of: *Three's Company*
Lasted: 14 months
Summary: a show essentially set in the living room of a boring older couple

The stars of this doomed spin-off, the Ropers, played the landlords in the original *Three's Company.* Mr. Roper was a crabby homebody, and his wife was a sex-crazed homebody, but the main focus in the original show were the Ropers' tenants, Jack Tripper and his two bouncingly cute female roommates. In the original show, there were all sorts of '70s hilarity about sex and the fact that Mr. Roper thought Jack was GAY—when he WASN'T! But with the spin-off, there wasn't even that amazingly hilarious gag— all there was were the Ropers. And a few dull new characters. Question: Who wants to see an older homebody at home with his older sex-starved homebody wife, episode after episode? Even after the producers desperately throw in a female boarder? (Answer: apparently a fair number—the show was still in the top 25 when it was canceled, which says more about the intellectual levels of the late '70s and early '80s than it does about the show.)

3. The Tortellis

Spin-off of: *Cheers*
Lasted: four months
Summary: Here's a not-very-promising idea: A spin-off about a sleazy character who runs a TV repair shop in Las Vegas.

Any moron can see that this is not one of those ideas that should have great appeal to its target Middle American TV audience. Apparently, television executives are different from the average American, because they liked the idea. The Nick Tortelli character had appeared on *Cheers,* the popular '80s show about a bar in Boston. Nick was the sleazy ex-husband of the witty and acerbic *Cheers* barmaid Carla. Here in this spin-off, instead of appearing every once in a while as a little bit of sleazoid seasoning, we have Nick as the sleazoid center of the show—along with a bimbo wife, a bimbo stupid son, and HIS bimbo wife. And instead of a cozy Boston bar as a backdrop, we have Las Vegas television repair. A show about a slimy lowlife who runs a Las Vegas TV repair shop, without any redeeming characteristics, surrounded by bimbos, is not a good idea. The public agreed.

4. Mayberry R.F.D.

Spin-off of: The Andy Griffith Show

Lasted: three years

Summary: one of the dullest shows in the world

The parent show, *The Andy Griffith Show*, was about a rural sheriff and life in North Carolina through his eyes. It centered around the sheriff's office and home. This spin-off was about a rural town councilman (played by mild-mannered Ken Berry) and life seen through his eyes. It centered around—the town-council office! Enough said. The show wasn't as bad as it was stultifyingly soporific. Old Aunt Bee had the most pep. Strangely enough, this show was very popular and was canceled only because the network wanted to get rid of rural-oriented shows.

5. The Bradys

Spin-off of: The Brady Bunch

Lasted: one month

Summary: utter bilge

A spin-off of itself. The parent show, *The Brady Bunch*, about a man with three boys marrying a woman with three girls and forming a very, very happy, happy family was bad (and popular) enough, but in this spin-off the Brady kids have grown up, and it's all much, much worse. The problem is that as adults they now have adult problems: alcoholism, coping with the AIDS scene, being a paraplegic, infertility. In fact, the Bradys had so many problems the show itself was extremely depressing to watch, so worried genius television executives had a brainstorm: They decided to put in a laugh track to cheer things up a bit. A show about paralyzed, alcoholic, or worried people with a background of hilarious TV canned laughter doesn't make it. And this show didn't.

6. The Girl from U.N.C.L.E.

Spin-off of: *The Man from U.N.C.L.E.*

Lasted: one season

Summary: sexist and stupid, even by notoriously vapid '60s standards

The Man from U.N.C.L.E., a campy and hip '60s spy show, was fun and a big hit; its spin-off, *The Girl from U.N.C.L.E.*, was not. Here's one reason: April Dancer (Stefanie Powers), the spy agency U.N.C.L.E.'s first female secret agent, was almost always RESCUED by her male counterpart, Mark Slate. She almost never fought her own battles. Worse, many plots revolved around April ALMOST GETTING MARRIED TO A BAD GUY! Of course, at the last minute, she'd be rescued by Mark Slate from this FATE WORSE THAN DEATH! With plots as advanced as this, it's no wonder the famous female TV spy of the '60s turned out to be Diana Rigg as Emma Peel of the Avengers—on another channel.

7. That '80s Show

Spin-off of: *That '70s Show*

Lasted: one season

Summary: took *That '70s Show* concept—life in the 1970s—and added a clever twist: life in the '80s

With ALL '80s THINGS! What a clever idea! And what about the title? How about . . . *That '80s Show*! Trouble was, the producers forgot to add plot, compelling characters, good jokes, acting talent, heart, zip. Some people complained the show even got '80s references wrong—it did sometimes, but the real problem was that the characters and plots (what there were of both) were so uncompelling and dull that all you could do to keep awake was to watch for those references. Clichéd characters (punker with a heart of gold); bad jokes (Permanent Record is the record store where one character works, but we modern in-the-know 2000s people know that records aren't permanent at all because CDs are coming soon, so we GET THE JOKE), annoying touches (including your now standard token one-dimensional bisexual), and too much clunk (clunky portable phones, so we can see how PRIMITIVE the '80s were!) Some people, mostly neurotic, aging TV critics, tried to like it; most thought it was a simply a dull procession of '80s products and songs. On the Web, someone summed up most audience's reactions: "I was excited to see the pilot at first, because, well, I love the eighties. [Then] I lost interest in it. . . . I wasn't aware it was canceled." When people forget whether you're even on or not, you've got a problem.

MTV's PROUD BROADCASTING FIRST— REAL EXCREMENT

CBS brought the news to broadcasting. MTV has now made its own contribution, a notable landmark in the history of television broadcasting: televised shit. And two teens were there to tell us about it. Both of them were from Big Bear Lake, California; they were among the audience at the Snow Summit Ski Resort, east of Los Angeles, in January 2001. Perhaps they thought they were lucky; they were near the stage when the Shower Rangers appeared during the filming of *Dude, This Sucks*. And that's when it began.

The Shower Rangers were onstage, standing before the audience. Then, they turned and pointed their naked butts to the audience. And then, in the words of the girls' lawyer, "Before they could say or do anything, the Shower Ranger whose buttocks faced them bent over, spread the cheeks of his buttocks and emitted a spray of fecal matter." Excrement was everywhere. According to one of the girls, "All of a sudden I was smelling something disgusting, and I started to gag. I looked around at my friends. They were covered in something. As I looked down at myself, I realized I was, too."

President of MTV Programming Brian Graden expressed regret over the "terrible incident" and, as befits a programmer working in the proud tradition of Edward R. Murrow, promised the segment would not be broadcast.

What Rock Stars Must Have Backstage

Here are some vital inclusions to musicians' backstage riders—lists of demands added to contracts, without which they, presumably, would be unable to perform:

- 4 pairs white tube socks (U.S. size 10–13)

12 cans of Cran beverages—from Ocean Spray or other reputable cranberry company

—Foo Fighters

- 10 pairs of white cotton crew socks and 10 cotton boxer shorts

   —Moby

- 4 red Fuji apples, . . . 1 kiwi fruit, 1 ripe papaya

   —Fiona Apple

- Two (2) boxes of cornstarch (VERY IMPORTANT)

   —Nine Inch Nails

- 24 peanut butter & jelly sandwiches

   —the Back Street Boys

- 1 fresh Wonder Bread (white)
  1 bottle Dom Pérignon chilled

   —Axl Rose, from Guns N' Roses

- One (1) box bendy straws

   —Mariah Carey

- Twelve (12) dozen freshly laundered bath-size towels and two (2) dozen black hand towels. . . . Please, no Pakistani compressed towels

   —Aerosmith

- Before serving, all food and ice must be inspected for hair, package, paper, etc. and all catering staff must wear hair nets

   —P. Diddy

- We are sad to have to make this comment but we will not tolerate the use of anything but fresh, clean, crushed, or cubed ice. NO FISH ICE! *If it had never happened, I wouldn't have to write this.*

  —Janet Jackson

- White room
  White flowers
  White tables / and or tablecloths
  White drapes
  White candles
  White couches
  White Lilies
  White Roses

  —Jennifer Lopez

- Both band rooms should have a "vibe" to them. It should feel like you are walking into a small apartment's. If these rooms are locker room's please pipe and base off the walls, using fabric with prints. Not just the standeed black or blue convention drape.

  —Korn

- 2 bunches of *fresh cut* mixed flowers to include the following: stargazer lilies, Casablanca's lilies, iris, gladiolas, and eucalyptus. Please provide a very limited amount of filler such as baby's breath, leaves, and ferns etc.

  —Dixie Chicks

Plain Bad TV Shows (That Weren't Sequels)

Cop Rock

Lasted: 11 episodes

A musical cop show with numbers like "I Want My Beemer Back," sung by a frustrated yuppie whose car has been impounded, sounds like a bomb.

Cop Rock was a big one.

The brainchild of Steve Bochco, who developed *Hill Street Blues,* it shows even television geniuses have their off moments. It was one of the most expensive show in TV history, with episodes costing about $1.8 million each (in 1990 dollars). It was very original, even compelling in a way— but too . . . weird . . . for audiences to like. It would have a tough scene, a crime, a trial, and then all of a sudden someone would burst out in song (jurors singing, "He's Guilty, guilty, guilty"; gang members rapping in the streets; the d.a. doing a song and dance in neon . . . very odd). Sometimes, the whole cast would dance.

To be sure, the show had its defenders. But not too many of them.

The worst epitaph for the show: On an episode of the campily sleazy *Married . . . with Children,* mother Peg Bundy warns her son, Bud, that if he doesn't settle down, she'll force him to watch *Cop Rock.* Bud settles down.

My Mother the Car

Lasted: one season (30 episodes)

Often voted the worst television show ever made— which is unfair to some later brilliant creations.

This terrible show was codeveloped by Allan Burns, who went on to create two hits: *The Mary Tyler Moore Show* and *Lou Grant*. *My Mother the Car* can be reduced to a Hollywood pitch by saying it was *Mister Ed* with a jalopy.

The show's title gives even the most vapid TV viewer a big clue to the main idea of the show. Shopping for a car, Dave Crabtree (Jerry Van Dyke) is strangely drawn to a 1928 used car with the sign "Fixer Upper." He buys it, and when he turns on the radio he hears his mom's voice: "Hello, Davey, it's your mother."

Of course, no one but Dave can hear Mom the car. Of course, Dave's family hates the old wreck of a car. And of course, there's a villain—a dastardly eccentric antique-car collector who wants the car. Most episodes center around these astonishingly clever story points: Dave trying to hide the fact that the car is his mom or else trying to thwart the mad collector—one of the duller forms of villain ever created. Somehow this vapid plot line made it past TV executives, but then again, this *was* the era of *The Beverly Hillbillies*. . . .

Turn-On

Lasted: one show

Halfway through the first episode, phone lines were clogged with angry viewers.

The sponsor, Bristol-Myers, cut ties to the show a little while later. Meanwhile, 75 affiliates of ABC, the network broadcasting the show, said they refused to air any more episodes—ever. This sounds like the making of a master bomb, which is exactly what *Turn-On* was.

The idea came from George Schlatter, the creator of the

'60s hit *Laugh-In*, a popular, funny (for the times) montage of skits, graphics, and comedy. *Turn-On* was supposed to be hipper, fresher, sexier—old-fashioned burlesque with modern humor, lots of quick cuts, and a superfast pace.

The result was nauseating—sometimes literally.

After NBC had turned it down flat, CBS tried it, but execs there claimed it actually made its test audiences physically "disturbed." Finally, ABC picked it up, and the disaster was now on their hands. It aired on Wednesday, February 5, 1969, after *Here Come the Brides*. Within minutes, *Turn-On* had angered, annoyed (and possibly nauseated) a large portion of the audience, much of it from Middle America—the sort of people who tend not to appreciate jokes about bestiality.

With graphics like RAPE IS FRIENDLIER THAN ARSON and TARZAN SWINGS WITH CHEETA appearing on the screen; with flashing SEX signs, cameras zooming in and out at odd angles, pulsating lights and futuristic music underlying bad sex jokes, this frenetic and tasteless show electrified audiences . . . the wrong way. It didn't take long to end the show; without a sponsor, with thousands of angry viewers calling or writing, with affiliates cutting ties to the show, ABC decided to "explore alternatives."

Emeril

Lasted: 7 episodes

You can almost hear the pitch: "Emeril Lagasse is the most popular chef on TV, so why not create an entire sitcom around his character; with all those viewers already, it *can't* fail."

The problem: It did fail.

The show was possibly the worst show in the history of electromagnetic communication; *My Mother the Car* had much more charm, and at least Jerry Van Dyke could act. Emeril proved he could talk loudly, but he couldn't act and should never try again in the interests of humanity. More to the point, the plots revolving around the master loudmouth chef were sophomoric. The show was so bad that after the pilot was shown to critics, one stood up and asked NBC West Coast president Scott Sassa, "Can you explain how a show like *Emeril* has gotten as far as it has? I'm not asking that facetiously. I'm trying to understand the process." The show was canceled, universally panned, after seven episodes.

Great Moments in Kiddie-Character Crime

Santa Claus, Mickey Mouse, Superman—we may no longer be kids, but these beloved characters of our childhood live on in our imaginations, in a wondrous, glittering fantasy world, far removed from the real world of violence, pain,

WHAT NETWORKS THINK ABOUT THEIR VIEWERS

ABC was excited about the success of Comedy Central's *The Man Show,* a classy program dedicated essentially to beer and breasts; so they got Jimmy Kimmel, the cocreator of that show, to come up with one for them, with a little difference. As an ABC memo put it, the original show "was targeted very specifically to young male alcoholics. This one will be much broader-based." With ideas and demographics like that, how can you go wrong?

and sordid street crime. Read these stories and relive the happy days of carefree youth . . .

Man assaults Cookie Monster

According to the man, it all started in a Sesame Place theme park in Langhorne, Pennsylvania, when he asked Cookie Monster to pose for a picture with his daughter. Cookie Monster instead "aggressively" put "a big blue paw" on his daughter's head—and pushed. The man got angry and allegedly then shoved and kicked the beloved blue monster; people all around started yelling, kids started crying, and the man was arrested. Sesame Street spokeswoman Audrey Shapiro confirmed that the incident took place, but she defended Cookie Monster: "Our characters do not act the way this man said," she commented. And then she added, "It is an honor to be Cookie Monster."

Santa robs a bank

It must have looked a bit odd to startled bank clerks at the Union Bank branch in Mission Valley, California. A bank robber complete with Santa hat and white beard loudly demanded money from frightened cashiers. Santa robbing banks—what was the world coming to? It turned out the bank robber in the Santa outfit was a former San Diego police officer, though police said he wasn't carrying a gun at the time.

Santa holds up tollbooth

In another case of Santa gone wrong, police in Houston were searching for a Santa who drove up to a tollbooth, wished the clerk a Merry Christmas, than brandished a gun and demanded all her money.

Windsurfing Santa nabbed at Niagara

Canadian John Fulton dresses up as Father Christmas and windsurfs the Niagara River every Christmas season to help support the homeless. Unfortunately, in 2002 strong winds blew him off course, into the American side of the river, where alert border-patrol guards nabbed him and took him into custody, only releasing him after he signed a form stating he had illegally entered the U.S.

Man roughs up Easter Bunny

A 21-year-old Wisconsin man was arrested for jumping an Easter Bunny at a Wausau mall. A man working as the mall Easter Bunny was greeting children when his assailant hopped on his lap, put him in a headlock, and punched him in the mouth—as the kiddies watched in horror. He was later arrested for bunny battering.

IT'S A MIRACLE!

Henry Newinn of Houston, Texas, president of the Worldwide Elvis Fan Club, reported in a press release his discovery in his very own backyard of a tree with a white patch of bark that resembled Elvis in profile.

Why Entertainers Should Avoid Throwing Anything into an Audience

Careful study of lawsuits has discovered a fascinating subset: that of objects thrown into audiences by entertainers.

In these cases, one must pity the poor multimillionaire entertainer—whether a talk-show host or a singer. In an effort to please the audience by throwing souvenirs, much like the crowd at SeaWorld tossing fish to seals, said entertainer is sometimes met not with adulation but with a pricey lawsuit.

The offensive objects:

T-shirt (thrown during The Tonight Show with Jay Leno)

During taping of the show, T-shirts were shot into the audience from an air gun. Most were pleased to get said T-shirt, but not Stewart Gregory of Cincinnati, Ohio. He claims he was (to use his words) "battered" and even "forcefully struck" when the shirt hit his eye. He filed suit against NBC, the show, and Jay Leno, asking for damages of more than $25,000 for "pain and suffering, disability, lost wages, emotional distress, humiliation and embarrassment."

Frisbee (thrown during a Kenny Rogers concert)

Singer Kenny Rogers was throwing a Frisbee during an event inside the ballroom at Dallas's Adams Mark Hotel when it hit a chandelier. The chandelier broke, and pieces hit an audience member, Kevin O'Toole—who sued Rogers for $2 million for injuries caused. His wife sued Rogers for $100,000, citing the deprivation of her husband's "services, love, guidance and companionship."

Cards with photo of celebrity on them (thrown by David Hasselhoff)

Hasselhoff was appearing on *The Rosie O'Donnell Show* when he threw a deck of cards emblazoned with his face into the audience. Judy Downey Fortson, claiming she was hit in the eye, filed suit. Saying that he "should have known that throwing cards into an audience could cause injury to the audience," she is seeking medical costs, lost and future earnings, and punitive damages.

The Top Nine Stupidest Things You Never Wanted to Know About Celebrities but They Feel Compelled to Tell You

Celebrities are fixtures on the talk-show circuit, usually offering fascinating, only partially scripted insights on what it was like working on the set of their last film. When this gets stale, celebrities often offer us totally *different* insights. . . .

9. Making love in the morning got me through morning sickness—I found I could be happy and throw up at the same time.

   —actress Pamela Anderson Lee

8. I didn't feel well earlier. That's why I fit into this dress. I was actually in the toilet all day.

   —actress Jennifer Lopez, who was wearing a very tight dress at the premiere party for *The Man in the Iron Mask*

7. I like my pussy. Sometimes I stare at it in the mirror when I'm undressing. I love my pussy. It is the complete summation of my life. . . . My pussy is the temple of learning.

—pop star Madonna

6. I woke up the next morning and looked over to see this guy looking absolutely horrified and petrified.

"What's wrong?" I said.

"You peed in the bed," he said.

That could well be the single most embarrassing moment of my life, even though it was a real good icebreaker for a new relationship.

—actress Jenny McCarthy, in her book, *Jen-X*

5. I was thinking about dying the other day. . . . The death thought came while I was sitting on my toilet peeing—that's where I have my most contemplative thoughts.

—pop star Madonna, in *Madonna: The Book*

4. When we measured heads in eighth grade, mine was the biggest.

—actress Marilu Henner

3. I'm obsessed with crocodiles and getting eaten by one. When I hear that someone's been eaten by a crocodile or shark, I just get all gooey. I start salivating.

—singer Tori Amos

2. I don't have any underwear on tonight.

   —actress Sally Kirkland during 1994 Oscar ceremony, to a
   reporter

1. When I got through with the twin pregnancy, my
   abdominal skin was such that I had to fold it up and
   then stick it in my pants.

   —actress Cybill Shepherd

Stupid Homes and Vacation Spots in the U.S.A.

America is famous for spacious skies and amber waves of grain. But we're not talking about those things here—rather, we've got peculiar tourist attractions, stale national parks, and weird homes.

Stupid House-Buying Tips

In the past few years, we've been real-estate crazy in the U.S.A. With low mortgage rates, people have been buying houses virtually sight unseen. Who cares what it is as long as it's a bargain and the price is going to go up tomorrow? However, there are times it behooves one to do some caring. There may, indeed, be some big problems. So, next time you go out and look for a house, be aware and follow these handy, helpful, reasonable tips from the world of American real estate:

House Buyer's Tip #1: Check for rotting cow carcasses in the backyard

Cathie Kunkle moved into her "dream house" in Ontario, California, without first asking herself this vital question: Is my backyard-to-be filled with rotting animal corpses? In her case, it would have been a good question, and the answer would have been "yes." It started for her after she had purchased the house, when she had contractors dig a backyard garden pond and they noticed a smell. . . . According to Kunkle, "At first we thought it was a dead chicken, but when they dug deeper they found more down there. The smell was horrendous." After digging, they found that "more" meant several enormous cow carcasses, all wrapped in plastic. Apparently, Kunkle's dream home was the site of an old dairy farm where the farmers had chosen to illegally bury the animals instead of sending them to a rendering yard. The entire development area of the Kunkle's home might in fact have been a giant illegal cow graveyard. According to Bob Feenstra, general manager of the Milk Producers Council, "It not the image dairymen want." It's also not the home Kunkle wants. She and her family stayed in a hotel while the dead cows were removed.

House Buyer's Tip #2: Check out the attic for mounds of raccoon dung

Scott and Marilee Suomela shelled out $600,000 for their house in Bloomfield Hills, outside Detroit, Michigan. Then they noticed a strange smell, coming from the attic. They soon found the source: half a ton of raccoon droppings— over 1,000 pounds (if you've forgotten what a ton weighs). In addition, they found two dead raccoons, as well as several live ones wandering around. The Suomelas' lawyer said, "Initially, my clients were devastated. This was a house they had looked forward to."

House Buyer's Tip #3: And how about bat guano?

Here's another one of those essential questions you sometimes just forget to ask. But for a couple in the southeastern United States (they wish to remain anonymous), this is one they should have remembered. After they had moved into their house, they found the air-conditioning wasn't working too well. They called in a repairman, who found that the central system wasn't venting properly. He went to the attic, and there he found the reason: bats. Thousands upon thousands of were living and dying—and excreting—up there. Their guano was clogging up the vents—and in fact was trickling down through the insulation and wood and penetrating the lower floors. Five 55-gallon containers' worth of bat guano were removed from the house. The couple moved out, though not before one of them developed a peripheral-vision disorder that apparently came from excessive exposure to bat guano and not before the entire bathroom floor fell in. . . . But that's another story.

House Buyer's Tip #4: Ask yourself: Is there anyone dead or mummified in my new home?

A man in the Lancaster, Pennsylvania, region recently bought a bargain house at a foreclosure sale. (The previous owner hadn't paid his mortgage bills.) When he opened the door to his wonderful bargain house, he discovered the reason the previous owner had not paid his mortgage bills: He couldn't sign any checks. How did the new owner discover this? He found the previous owner's naturally mummified body with a pile of bills near the front-door mail slot. How the bank missed the body and the very good excuse for mortgage delinquency is unknown.

House Buyer's Tip #5: Ask the owners: When you say you're selling the house, just what exactly do you mean?

Here we get into a tricky definitional problem. And the answer is Clintonesque: It depends on what the meaning of the word "house" is. One couple, buying their new home, discovered this ambiguity the hard way. It seems the seller of their house had a very strict sense of what a "house" is: It means the house, period. Not the lightbulbs, cabinet knobs in the kitchen and shop, nor any electrical fixtures, and no, not even the plastic switch covers, and not any built-in drawers, and not any stray pieces of wall-to-wall carpeting, either (large chunks had been cut away), no curtain rods, and no, no appliances. (Here the previous owner was a little generous. He *replaced* all of the appliances with old ones that didn't work. But at least they filled the spaces.) The seller's family removed all of these things just before the closing. In addition, the previous owner siphoned all of the oil out of the fuel tank, after the gauge had been read for the closing adjustment. At least there was no bat guano.

House Buyer's Tip #6: Ask: Are the windows in the right way? And: Are the floorboards nailed down?

Here's some home-contracting wisdom: The basic idea of a window is to keep things like rain out. Windows put in backward tend not to do that too well. And don't forget: when using wood—also use nails. Karen Groceman learned the hard way that the developers who built her house had kind of slacked off a bit on these finer points. First, she noticed her cats licking the window joints in her new Lee's Summit home, near Kansas City, Missouri, on a rainy day. She was puzzled. Then she realized: Water was pouring in through the windows because the ace contractors had put them in backward. Her problems didn't stop there: When she called to complain, the developers sent a crew to fix things. But the crew didn't have any tools. They asked if they could borrow hers. As she told *The Kansas City Star,* they proceeded to bang the windows up, only making the problems worse. Then she noticed that the floors weren't nailed down—and the roof was sagging, too, more than three inches, because there weren't enough braces. Groceman and her husband went to a county arbitrator, who said that the developer hadn't supervised the building subcontractor very well. One thing, though, they made the house look good. As Karen Groceman put it, "The house was beautiful. We walked in and said, 'Wow.' " Then, in one of the understatements of the year, she added, "It just wasn't built very well."

House Buyer's Tip #7: See how many jet fighters maneuver after midnight near your house

It's one of those things you sometimes just forget. And one "smart" house hunter didn't bother asking. He noticed that a new home had been on the market more than a year. Cleverly, he thought he'd go directly to the builder, bypassing the greedy real-estate agents, and get a real bargain. He sure did. On one of his first nights in his new home, he was awakened by a deafening roar. He leaped out of bed and went outside and looked up. He then saw not one jet fighter, but an entire squadron of them streaking across the sky. His sky; the sky above his home. His bargain house was located right beneath a jet-fighter flight-training area. The next night, the same thing happened, but now he knew. And it wasn't so bad. The military practiced only fifteen nights a month. And for only $70 a night, he could spend those nights at a nearby motel.

Stupid Official State "Things"

Never let it be said that our state legislators don't do a bang-up job of making sure that the important things are legislated—things like making sure that the state recognizes just the *right* flying mammal or cooking pot as worthy of honor.

Thing	Official State What?	Where
pecan	official state health nut	Texas
teddy bear	official state toy	Mississippi
grits	official state prepared food	Georgia
Antigo silt loam	official state grass	Texas
armadillo	official state small mammal (the longhorn is the official state mammal)	Texas
coal	official state rock	Utah
Dutch oven	official state cooking pot	Utah
Mexican free-tailed bat	official state flying mammal	Texas
bluebunch wheatgrass	official state grass	Washington
Pacific golden chanterelle	official state mushroom	Oregon
fiddle	official state musical instrument	South Dakota

Thing	Official State What?	Where
kuchen	official state dessert	South Dakota
Nokota	official state equine	North Dakota
tule duck decoy	official state artifact	Nevada
spotted newt	official state amphibian	New Hampshire
"New Mexico—Mi Lindo Nuevo Mexico"	official state bilingual song	New Mexico
Tennessee cave salamander	official state amphibian	Tennessee
Red or green?	official state question	New Mexico
eastern black walnut	official state tree nut	Missouri
Typic argiustolls, Holdrege series	official state soil	Nebraska
prehistoric whale	official state fossil	Mississippi
jousting	official state sport	Maryland
Maine coon cat	official state cat	Maine
cranberry juice	official state beverage	Massachusetts

Stupid Battle over State Cookie: Chocolate Chip or Sugar?

The Pennsylvania State Senate and House were locked in a battle in the spring of 2003 over this vital question: What should the state cookie be? Senate Bill 320 calls for chocolate chip to be the state cookie. But the House is pushing for the Nazareth sugar cookie; the argument is that Nazareth, Pennsylvania, where the cookie originated, provided "much of the stimulus for the founding, settlement and growth" of Pennsylvania. "Besides," says one sponsor, sugar cookies are "appetite pleasers, a means of communication, and can be used for bartering." Bartering?

⭐

A KINDER, GENTLER AMERICA

Several cushy, affluent towns in California, among them Rolling Hills Estates on the Palos Verdes peninsula, were ordered to meet state-mandated requirements for low-income housing. Their solution? They counted all maids and servant's quarters on their estates as low-income housing.

Chocolate supporters counter that Pennsylvania leads the United States in chocolate production and that Pennsylvanians have a "steadfast and loyal devotion" to the chocolate-chip cookie.

"To be honest, I'd be much more concerned with passing a state budget than a state cookie," one state senator summed up. "But if I were promoting a cookie, I'd say it would have to be the Oreo."

Cities That Are Advertising

It's a very American thing: naming a city or town after a product to help push sales. Two cases in point: First, eBay offshoot Half.com decided that a good way to get publicity would be to convince Halfway, Oregon, to change its name to Half.com. The town of about 360 people (though more than 2,000 if one includes the surrounding region) put through a temporary name change—the city would still "officially" be Halfway. The city gained 20 computers for its elementary school, a free city website, and "seed money" for economic development ($73,000 in 2000 and another $20,000 in 2001) for the change.

More recently, the California Milk Processor Board—the

people responsible for the "Got Milk?" campaign—started looking for a small town to call their own. Or rather, to *rename* itself Got Milk, California. The board sent out milk cartons stuffed with a GOT MILK? T-shirt and a letter to the mayors of 20 small towns, hoping that someone would agree to change their community's name in exchange for having a Got Milk? museum built (a tourism attraction) and getting a substantial contribution to local schools. As of October 2002, there were still no takers. The mayor of Biggs, California (population 1,793), responded but was flooded by media calls . . . and is now thinking it's a long shot. Other cities still are (theoretically) considering it.

Fascinating Names of Cities

Americans are a creative bunch, as may be gathered from the names of some of the cities, towns, and burgs in which we live. The following are all U.S. towns (however, not all of them are incorporated) and all are a bit . . . unusual. . . .

Muck City, Alabama	*Toad Suck, Arkansas*
Chicken, Alaska	*Wiener, Arkansas*
Eek, Arizona	*Bummerville, California*
Nowhere, Arizona	*Fruityland, California*
Why, Arizona	*Poopout Hill, California*
Blue Ball, Arkansas	*Wimp, California*
Nimrod, Arkansas	*ZZYZX, California*

Dick, Colorado

Hygiene, Colorado

Blue Ball, Delaware

Two Egg, Florida

Between, Georgia

Climax, Georgia

Santa Claus, Georgia

Papa, Hawaii

Poopoo, Hawaii

Bitch Creek, Idaho

Bitch Lake, Idaho

Normal, Illinois

Gas City, Indiana

Gnaw Bone, Indiana

Munster, Indiana

Diagonal, Iowa

Ogle, Kentucky

Ordinary, Kentucky

Typo, Kentucky

Waterproof, Louisiana

Beans Corner Bingo, Maine

Boring, Maryland

Hell, Michigan

Podunk, Michigan

Embarrass, Minnesota

Welcome, Minnesota

Arm, Mississippi

Dick, Mississippi

It, Mississippi

Bland, Missouri

Dick, Missouri

Enough, Missouri

Peculiar, Missouri

Useful, Missouri

Offer, Montana

Two Dot, Montana

Bee, Nebraska

Worms, Nebraska

Jackpot, Nevada

Bivalve, New Jersey

Organ, New Mexico

Tingle, New Mexico

Bitch Mountain, New York

Result, New York

Surprise, New York

Duck, North Carolina

Meat Camp, North Carolina

Whynot, North Carolina

Zap, North Dakota

River Styx, Ohio

Pink, Oklahoma

Boring, Oregon

Idiotville, Oregon

Zigzag, Oregon

Drab, Pennsylvania

Laboratory, Pennsylvania

Panic, Pennsylvania

Coward, South Carolina

Oral, South Dakota

Porcupine, South Dakota

Disco, Tennessee

Dismal, Tennessee

Finger, Tennessee

Static, Tennessee

Sweet Lips, Tennessee

Cut and Shoot, Texas

Ding Dong, Texas

Noodle, Texas

Oatmeal, Texas

Telephone, Texas

Wink, Texas

Virgin, Utah

Assawoman, Virginia

Fries, Virginia

Index, Washington

Hoo Hoo, West Virginia

Man, West Virginia

Odd, West Virginia

Embarrass, Wisconsin

Imalone, Wisconsin

Ubet, Wisconsin

WHAT'S IN A NAME....

The city council of the town of Little Booger Creek decided to go back to the town's old name of Town Creek in 2001. The reason: The city fathers wanted to apply for a federal grant for a creekside hiking and biking trail and decided that Little Booger Creek wouldn't look too good on federal aid papers.

Tourism Marvels

The U.S. is known for its many tourist destinations—from large cities such as New York and Los Angeles to theme parks such as Walt Disney World and natural attractions, from the mountains to the prairies....

You get the idea.

What of those cities and towns that need to drum up business on their own? There are cases where American ingenuity must be exercised.

Giant Lava Lamp

Soap Lake, Washington—a 1,700-population town—used to be a popular tourist destination. To start drawing the crowds back, the city council has embarked on a revitalization plan. First move: Building a 60-foot-tall Lava lamp on Main Street. One of the prime movers of the plan explained: "I just for some reason thought of [a] lava lamp."

Frozen Corpse

One-hundred-and-one-year-old—and frozen—Grandpa Bredo is the draw in Nederland, Colorado. The man died in 1989, and his grandson, a follower of cryonics, had him frozen, hoping he could one day be thawed. Each month, a caretaker packs the corpse with fresh dry ice—and once a year, he is the center of the town's Frozen Dead Guy Days, a festival that includes coffin races and viewings of Grandpa Bredo . . . in the shed in the backyard where he is kept.

Big Nuts

Two different towns boast extremely large nuts. The world's largest pecan is in Brunswick, Missouri (outside the Nut Hut). The pecan replica was built in 1985 by pecan farmers George and Elizabeth James to advertise their patented Starking Hardy Giant pecan. It weighs 12,000 pounds and is 7 by 12 feet. The world's second-largest pecan is in Seguin, Texas (in front of city hall). Built in 1962 by a dentist with civic pride, it was dedicated to Spanish explorer Cabeza de Vaca who was held captive on the Guadalupe River for ten years and subsisted on the local pecans. Weighing in at a mere 1,000 pounds (and standing at 5 by 2½ feet, it is not truly the world's largest pecan, city still calls itself "Home of the World's Largest Pecan" and sells postcards of the pecan.

Giant Chee-to

A "naturally large" Chee-to was initially found in a Cheetos bag in Hawaii by Naval Petty Officer Mike Evans. Evans tried to auction it on eBay, but disc jockey Bryce Wilson read about the snack online . . . and lobbied to have it brought to his town, Algona, Iowa, as a tourist draw. The giant Chee-to—slightly smaller than a tennis ball (but much larger than the average Chee-to), weighs only three fifths of an ounce "but has quite a girth," according to Wilson. The Chee-to came to town in a motorcade and was unveiled before a cheering crowd of 200. The unveiling was also broadcast on *The Jimmy Kimmel Show*. It is now on display in a glass case at Sister Sarah's Restaurant in Algona.

Toilet-Paper Show in the World Capital of Toilet Paper

In 2002, a unique exhibition opened in Green Bay, Wisconsin: "Privy to the Past: Inside America's Most Private Room." Green Bay was no idle choice for this exhibition about bathrooms; according to the museum spokesperson, Green Bay is "the toilet paper capital of the world." The exhibition included all sorts of precursors to modern toilet paper and showed how pre-1935 toilet paper used to have splinters in it. According to the spokesperson, "That would have been very painful." This exhibition was sponsored by, appropriately enough, Georgia-Pacific, makers of Quilted Northern Bath Tissue.

Want to Breathe Polluted Air? Come to the U.S. Park System

Ozone levels in the Great Smokey Mountains exceeded federal standards 175 times between 1998 and 2002—rivaling the *city* of Los Angeles. So you want clean air, go to New York City! You want pollution, come to the great American outdoors! Here's a list of some of the most polluted national parks in the United States, for those of us who want a nature vacation with a twist or a hacking cough. . . .

1. *Acadia National Park, Maine*
   Pollution: ozone, acid rain and residue, mercury, "degraded scenic vistas"

2. *Everglades National Park, Florida*
   Pollution: highest mercury readings in water and soil recorded *anywhere* in America (except maybe for certain apartment buildings in Hoboken, New Jersey).

3. *Glacier National Park, Montana*
   Pollution: not much—it's just with all that global warming, there isn't that much in the way of glaciers anymore

4. *Great Smokey Mountains, North Carolina*
   Pollution: ozone, ozone, and more ozone. The most polluted national park in America. To be fair, recent scientific studies show that the reason for this may be all the trees—which release gases that convert to ozone. Park officials are concerned that all the ozone is damaging the respiratory systems of park workers, visitors, and all the little animals that live in the park

5. *Mammoth Cave National Park, Kentucky*
   Pollution: a double whammy—some of the highest levels of ozone in the air and mercury everywhere else

6. *Sequoia and Kings Canyon Parks, California*
   Pollution: this park has the largest trees in the world—and large amounts of pesticides in the groundwater and ozone in the air. Average annual ozone is *worse* than that in New York City, Houston, Chicago, or Atlanta

7. *Shenandoah National Park, Virginia*
   Pollution: a diverse botanical reserve with acid rain
   pouring out of the sky. The pH of the groundwater
   has even changed.

The Idiot Next Door

We are happy to report that stupidity and the committing of stupid acts is not something restricted to the rich, the famous, the powerful, or the institutional.

No, in the spirit of American democracy, stupid acts can be committed by *any* of us. This section celebrates this: the stupidity of the masses—the idiots next door, if you will. (Rest assured, we are not speaking of you, however.)

Awe-Inspiring Freelance Amateur Stupidity

Among us are geniuses, true; but there are also thousands of people who stand in dire need—not of more brains but of *any* brains.

Woman convinced dog-costumed thief is stealing her roses

A Cupertino, California, woman kept noticing that roses were being taken from her yard. First, she blamed squirrels. But when she heard a crash and saw the rear end of a dog leaving the scene of the crime, she came to a new, logical conclusion: A thief dressed like a dog (to avoid identification) had been stealing her roses. Why would someone be disguised as a dog? It makes perfect sense, or so she says: "A dog can go anywhere and nobody will be suspicious." Now we get it.

Man photocopies his butt in crowded courthouse lobby

In an attempt to play a practical joke on his girlfriend, a 38-year-old Missouri man (allegedly) dropped his pants in the lobby of the St. Louis County Courthouse and began making photocopies of his buttocks. When police arrived, he already had made two copies and was in the process of making a third. "What did I do? What did I do?" he asked— as the cops arrested him.

Dairy Queen worker accepts $200 bill, gives $197 in change

A clerk at the Dairy Queen in Danville, Kentucky, accepted a $200 bill from a customer who bought $2.12 worth of food. The customer received her change and drove away. Not only is there no such thing as a $200 bill, but the note in question had on the back an oil well, while on the front was a portrait of George W. Bush, and on the White House lawn were signs reading: WE LIKE BROCCOLI and ROOMS NOT FOR RENT.

Man hires hit man, tries to pay in cows

Maybe it's not so stupid, really. What if you need a hit arranged but are low on money? Find out what else you have. This is what a 64-year-old farmer in Alaska did in 2001; he wanted a hit on his best friend's ex-wife (why? don't ask) and, of course, instead of finding a real hit man managed to contact an undercover cop. But the odd part about it was the price he agreed to pay: $300 cash and four cows on the hoof.

Protester chains himself to wrong fence

In 2003, a young Washington State man decided to protest the war on Iraq in a dramatic and decisive way: He'd chain himself to the entrance of the local office of the U.S. Department of Energy and block access. So he did just that, effectively blocking workers from entering or leaving. He told passersby he was doing this to protest Bush's foreign and domestic policies and the war in Iraq. The young man probably noticed that people, instead of showing either anger or support, were more puzzled than anything else. For good reason: the building he was blocking wasn't the U.S. Department of Energy. The protester was dramatically blocking the doors to the Grange, a nongovernment, nonprofit farmer's organization dedicated to helping rural people—keeping workers from doing things like working to lower seed prices for farmers.

Census taker finds no one at home, so does the logical thing

A very diligent North Carolina census taker—maybe we should say an *over*diligent North Carolina census taker—was trying to deliver a census form to a home in Gastonia, near Charlotte. He knocked and knocked, and he rang and rang, and he came back three times, but no one ever answered. Once, he even left the form tucked under a screen door, but no one ever filled it out. So he broke into their house—and left the form on the kitchen table. As it was, there was someone home, a young girl on the telephone. And so the census taker was arrested and charged with breaking and entering.

Woman opens spray can with electric can opener

A woman from Leonia, New Jersey, in February 2003 suffered second- and third-degree burns from a fire which broke out when she tried to open a spray paint can with an electric can opener. Fire officials were uncertain if a spark from the can opener set off the flame. The woman did not explain why she was trying to open the spray can with a can opener in the first place.

Men engage in "hairy" knife fight

Police from Mansfield Township and Hackettstown, New Jersey, arrested a man, charging him with aggravated assault after he allegedly slashed his friend's face during a fight. The fight broke out after they began arguing over the time-honored question, Who has the most hair on his buttocks?

Bank teller deposits million-dollar bill

A woman approached a not-amazingly-astute teller at the First National City Bank of Newport, in Harrisburg, Pennsylvania. She gave the teller a single bill—a million-dollar bill. The teller didn't bat an eye—just took the bill and credited the woman's account for one million dollars. (For the record, the largest denomination note in circulation is the $100 bill.)

America's Garage Sale: Stupid eBay Auctions

It is said that eBay has changed the American consumer marketplace.

Many odd things have been sold on eBay—from towns

GREAT MOMENTS IN FREE SPEECH

It's a basic right, as set forth by the Founding Fathers, or Founding Parents, as the case may be: freedom of speech, the freedom to express yourself in the ways you see fit.

A man from Washington State has visually demonstrated this right guaranteed by our Bill of Rights by carving a 6-foot tree stump into the shape of a penis, topped by two American flags. He also plans to cover it with a giant condom at some point—to promote safe sex. On Christmas, he intends to move it to his porch and decorate it with Christmas lights.

Neighbors have complained, but according to the county police, "People have the right to have poor taste. We don't have a county ordinance that I know of that says you can't carve your tree into a penis."

(Bridgeville and Carlotta, California, sold for $1.8 million and $1.065 million respectively; another town, Amboy, California, didn't sell as the reserve price wasn't met) to submarines to taxidermy items such as a petrified boar's heart (which didn't sell, as again the reserve price was not met).

But here, we speak not of towns (however wonderful Bridgeville and Carlotta may be) nor even of taxidermy items (however compelling the notion of a petrified boar's heart may be to the collector) but of the more offbeat auctioned items, many of which beg the question: Who is stupider—the person putting the item up for auction or the one who bids on it?

First, the legitimate, if somewhat odd, ones . . .

Item: 16-inch diamond necklace that had been swallowed by a jewel thief . . . and reemerged in his bowel movement

Minimum bid: $75,000
High bid: n/a but expected to make over $100,000

Harold's Jewelers owner Lee Mendelson of Boca Raton, Florida, had been robbed—but the merchandise was recovered when police caught the thief and saw the stolen diamond necklace and two loose diamonds in an X ray. Mendelson decided to put the necklace—with 83 diamonds and weighing nearly 30 carats—up for auction after the theft got a great deal of press, including numerous jokes on talk shows. He also noted—to quell any fears about cleanliness—that it had been boiled in alcohol, run through a jewelry-cleaning machine, and boiled again in a borax solution.

Item: Justin Timberlake's French toast
Minimum bid: $1.00
High bid: $1,025.00

This was put up for sale by radio station Z100 with the proceeds going to charity. The description: "This is Justin Timberlake of N*SYNC'S leftover french toast as eaten live in Z100!!! The entire group was on the Z-Morning Zoo this morning, March 9th, and Justin only ate one bite of his french toast! You'll get his half-eaten french toast, fork he used, and the plate . . . complete with extra syrup!" While bids actually went higher (up to over $3,000), Z100 noted that any bids over $1,000 that couldn't be confirmed by phone would be canceled. So the breakfast ultimately went for a mere $1,025—sold to a University of Wisconsin sophomore who said she "just wanted a piece of them."

Item: Donny Osmond's nachos
Minimum bid: $1.00
High bid: $22.43

These were nachos that Donny Osmond was eating during a June 29, 2001, concert—and that he didn't finish. The description noted: "If you look closely, you can see where a chip has broken off in the cheese." One may note Osmond's food didn't scale the same heights as Timberlake's. . . .

Item: false teeth and original teeth
Minimum bid: $2.00
High bid: $34.77
Let us allow the item description written by the eBay seller to speak for itself:

Whacky and weird! Great for gags or Dental display or to just gross someone out! This is a set of false teeth and the original teeth that my mother had pulled from her mouth more than 50 years ago. Just as they came from her mouth when the dentist pulled them,—original teeth are in pouch for safekeeping. Don't ask me why she saved them, but it's time to downsize homes, so space is limited and out they go. Will be a true find for some lucky person!

Apparently, there were a number of people who hoped to get lucky—the teeth got 12 bids over the 7-day auction.

Item: tampon guardian angels . . . real cute
Minimum bid: $0.25
High bid: $0.25
A somewhat different craft item—two small angels hand-made from tampons—that never got past the minimum-bid amount. (Shipping and handling was $2 and the lucky winner could also have them insured for only $1.30.) The description referred to the angels as "little cuties" and "little

darlings"—and also suggested that they would make a great gift "for a lady with a sense of humor."

Item: boxes for two handheld computers
Minimum bid: $3.99
High bid: none

One hopeful person put up two handheld-computer boxes (or as it was typed on eBay, "Boxs")—one for a Visor Platinum and the other for a Visor Deluxe. The detailed description noted that the Platinum box had a photo of the computer on the cover, some paper torn off (about 1 inch by ½ inch), and some scratches but still "is in very good condition." The Visor Deluxe box was said to be in excellent condition. Surprisingly, there were no bids.

Item: Bernese mountain dog hair sheddings
Minimum bid: $5.00
High bid: $10.00

"Freshly gathered from various locations around our home. 99% black in color with small amounts of white and light-brown hairs." This item garnered four bids—and the lucky winner paid only $10. . . . plus appropriate shipping-and-handling charges.

Item: potato that looked (or so the auctioneer claimed) like Jennifer Lopez
Minimum bid: $0.01
High bid: $18.50

"PotaLo"—as the auctioneer called this potato—is "one hundred percent Idaho spud." The lucky winner received not only the potato but also three photos of it in a white hat, in a bikini, and as "Nude PotaLo on Black Mink."

Item: urologist's testicle sizer

Minimum bid: $12.00

High bid: $12.00 (sold through the "Buy It Now" feature)

As one might ascertain, this item was a testicle measurer—or more specifically a "*real life* testicle sizer used by urologists," as the seller noted, also suggesting that, by purchasing this, "you can size up the testicles of your loved ones."

Item: septorhinoplasty surgery

Minimum bid: $3,500.00 (or "Buy It Now" for $7,000.00)

High bid: n/a

The seller explained that the item up for bid was a "complete surgical procedure for Septorhinoplasty"... also commonly known as a "nose job." While the winning bid would have included all medical fees (including hospital, surgery, equipment, and anesthesia) and the procedure would have been performed by one of the "premier Ear Nose Throat surgeons in Idaho, with over 25 years experience," there were no bids at all.

And the pranks and hoaxes ...

These are eBay listings that were found to be spurious, fraudulent, or otherwise ridiculous and were pulled from the auction site. You can see how eBay came to these conclusions. ...

Item: one human soul (listed by two different people two different times)

Minimum bid: $0.99

High bid: n/a

Soul #1 was listed in 2002 by 20-year-old Adam Burtle—and bidding reached $400 before the auction was pulled. Soul #2 was listed by 24-year-old Nathan Wright of West Des Moines (who also wanted to get publicity for his online magazine)—and was housed in a glass jar that "may or may not" have contained fudge prior to the soul. Wright said he was considering selling his morality at a later date.

Item: family: husband and wife, two children (ages 8 and 9)

Minimum bid: $5 million

High bid: none

California writer Steve Young put his family on eBay after reading about a town for sale. His thought: "If a town could be sold online, then how much could you get for a family?" In his seller's comments, he noted that the winner would receive a lifetime of platonic commitment (including invitations to family outings and holiday get-togethers as well as helpful hints about writing, gardening, and cooking) and that the family would relocate anywhere. In addition, the two older Youngs would change their last name to whatever the high bidder wanted. The ad got more than 10,000 hits minutes after it was placed on a Thursday—but eBay pulled it the next day, explaining that it is against policy to sell human beings. As eBay spokesman Kevin Pursglove said, "People have tried to sell themselves five or six times over the past four or five years. There have been attempts to sell their nephew, uncle, wife, whoever is in the doghouse at the time. They've even tried to sell their soul."

Item: human kidney

Minimum bid: $2.5 million

High bid: $5.75 million

One of the most famous eBay auctions, in this case a man listed a "fully functional kidney for donation" under the category "Miscellaneous: General." The listing noted that he was willing to donate the kidney for a "reciprical [*sic*] donation of 2.5 million dollars to a charity of my choice" and that the kidney recipient was expected to pay all medical expenses for both parties. The posting was pulled—but not until bidding had already reached nearly $6 million—and later eBay noted that the offer probably was a hoax.

Item: another (cheaper) human kidney
Minimum bid: $250,000
High bid: n/a

In this case—years after the above kidney was listed—a Rossville, Georgia, man offered one of his kidneys to the highest bidder, writing in the item description: "I am a white male, 44 years old, in excellent health and wish to sell one of my kidneys for $250,000 plus all expenses. My blood type is O-negative. Serious inquiries only." Again, eBay removed the posting hours after it was first up and stated that it believed it was a prank.

Item: human testicle
Minimum bid: $100.00
High bid: n/a

A simple offering—one human testicle . . . but one that apparently didn't grasp the imagination of eBay browsers, as it received no bids.

Item: spy plane
Minimum bid: $1 million

High bid: $100 million

In 2000, a U.S. spy plane popped onto eBay—its description saying that "this is USA spy plane that was in collision with my country Chinese jet fighter." The auctioneer also noted that the winner was "responsible for picking up plane." It turned out to be a prank, played by the hosts of Tampa, Florida–based *MJ Morning Show*—but eBay didn't catch on for about a day. The item remained up and got no bids for nearly 24 hours, but then action heated up—ultimately reaching $100 million before it was pulled.

Item: vote in the 2000 election
Minimum bid: $5.00
High bid: $10,100.00

A disgruntled Maryland voter put his vote up for sale on eBay to protest political corruption. The item listing: "The 2000 election vote of one U.S. citizen who is a registered voter in Maryland in the United States. You may specify whom I vote for in the presidential and all other elections in my district, by name or by party. Why should the American citizen be left out? Congressmen and senators regularly sell their votes to the highest bidder. Democracy for sale!" After 20 bids, the value of his vote had reached $10,100.

Item: young man's virginity
Minimum bid: $10.00
High bid: $10 million

A young man stated in his item description that he was a high school senior and had "decided I'd like to lose my virginity. I figured with the latest e-Bay craze, I'd see exactly how much I could get for my virginity." He also noted that he was in the top 5% of his class, a member of the National

Honor Society, and president of his school's computer and AV clubs, among other accomplishments.

> *Item:* 200 pounds of pure, uncut cocaine
> *Minimum bid:* $2 million
> *High bid:* $2 million

"That's right! 200 pounds of everyone's favorite white drug! Only available for a short time, get your 8 ball today!" said the item description . . . which included a photograph of the coke. This auction was pulled 18 hours after it was listed.

Five Unusually Stupid Criminals

There are so many stupid criminals out there that one must sometimes wonder how criminals manage to pull off any crimes successfully. That said, here are five who most definitely fall in the unsuccessful category.

Robber robs a Taco Bell—then orders a chalupa

A robber rode into a drive-in Taco Bell in Fort Worth, Texas, and demanded all the cash from the register. Then, maybe feeling hungry from all this effort, instead of pedaling off on his bike he decided to stay a while—and so he ordered a chalupa. While he was waiting, the police came and arrested him.

Thief leaves his wallet at scene of crime

A Lantana, Florida, thief had everything worked out for his crime—and it all ran smoothly. He opened his wallet and asked a gas-station clerk for change . . . then, when the reg-

FASCINATING NAMES OF PEOPLE

According to an article in the *Santa Cruz Sentinel,* the following are among their residents:

Climbing Sun

Shalom Dreampeace Compost

Chip

Darting Hummingbird Over a Waterfall

Moonbeam Moonbeam

XXXXXXXX X

ister was open, put his wallet on the counter, pulled a gun, and asked for all the money. He left with about $200. Unfortunately, he *didn't* leave with his wallet, which was still on the counter. When the cops arrived, they looked through the wallet, found traffic citations the thief had received, and tracked his car—to the parking lot of the thief's apartment complex—where he was arrested.

Lack of onion rings foils crime

A not amazingly astute man walked into a Burger King in Ypsilanti, Michigan, just before 8:00 A.M., flashed a gun, and demanded cash. The clerk said he couldn't open the cash register to get the money without a food order. So the man ordered onion rings. The clerk said they weren't available for breakfast. So the man with the gun . . . walked away.

Shy bank robber loses nerve

He's been dubbed the "world's wimpiest bank robber." A man in his 20s, wearing a baseball cap, went to a Long Island branch of HSBC, walked over to a bank cashier, and handed her a note demanding $40. The clerk looked at the note and at him and said, "Are you for real?" The bank robber sheepishly nodded his head, but the clerk didn't react. So the would-be robber just took back his note and walked away.

Jewelry thief attempts robbery during cop convention

Another idiot thief decided to rob a jewelry store in Ogden, Utah. Unfortunately for this thief, he picked the wrong day. Dozens of motorcycle cops were in town for an international convention, and when a few dozen of them heard cries for help from the jewelry clerk, they did what motorcycle cops do best: They hopped on their motorcycles and set off in pursuit. The poor thief was knocked into a wall, handcuffed, and hauled off to jail.

Stupidest Crimes Ever Committed by a Stupidity Expert

Writer James Welles wrote two books on stupidity—*The Story of Stupidity* and *Understanding Stupidity*. Perhaps he needed to reread his own works. He was arrested for soliciting sex from a 15-year-old "girl" (actually a 40-year-old Lantana, Florida, police detective) he met online. After three weeks of correspondence, including the notable e-mail in which Welles wrote, "You just have to remember—bottom line, I'll be committing a crime," he arranged to meet the girl at a Denny's restaurant. He was arrested when he showed up for his date.

Some Different Computer Crimes

There are those who are involved in computer fraud, hacking, and the like—making millions of dollars utilizing technology.

Then there is the schlub next door who is involved in a somewhat different form of computer crime. Four of the best examples:

1. Man arrested for shooting computer

Many of us have gotten frustrated with our computers. Few take it to the length that James Tourville of Oxford, Michigan, did. Annoyed with his computer, he started shooting at it. He wounded the computer, yes—but, unfortunately, he also wounded his next-door neighbor. He was arrested.

2. Another man arrested for shooting computer

A bar owner and sportsman in Lafayette, Colorado, had had enough of computer crashes. While customers at his Sportsman's Inn Bar and Restaurant watched, he shot his laptop computer four times, hung it on the wall as a hunting trophy—then was arrested and jailed on suspicion of felony menacing, reckless endangerment, and the prohibited use of weapons. He said in the police report that, after he had time to think, he realized he shouldn't have shot his computer. But at the time, it seemed like the right thing to do.

3. Man arrested for sledgehammering computer

It was a matter of taking customer service into his own hands. . . . A Grand Chute, Wisconsin, man had taken his daughter's new computer back to the Gateway store to be repaired five times in three months. He had had a run of problems with the hard drive, the sound card, and the CD drive. And the time had come to make a stand. So he went to the local Gateway Country computer shop, put the computer on the counter, then went and got a sledgehammer from his car, and started smashing the computer repeatedly. "I said, 'Have a good day,' and I left," he said. Police arrested him later and charged him with disorderly conduct. But the man seemed unrepentant—indeed, relieved. He said, "I wonder how many people are out there complaining and not getting service. It feels good in a way."

4. Man reports very peculiar computer theft

A Cullman, Alabama, man called the cops to report a theft: His hard drive had been stolen! He realized this after his computer stopped working properly. He wanted to let the cops know his theory: Someone had stolen his hard drive—and replaced it with a less efficient one.

Stupid 911 Calls

Making a 911 call seems a simple thing to grasp: You call 911 for an emergency—a fire, say, or a heart attack. You push the digits 9-1-1 and state the emergency. Very easy.

But however simple it seems, there are those Americans who don't seem to have *quite* gotten the gist of it. This is demonstrated by the following actual 911 calls, many of which were collected by 911 dispatchers for their own amusement.

> *Caller:* I call 911 and they give me the number, is that right?
>
> *Operator:* No ma'am, it's 411 for information.

. . . . .

> *Caller:* There's a gentleman that keeps parking in handicapped parking, and he's not handicapped.

. . . . .

> *Caller:* I need to talk to somebody concerning some graffiti in my neighborhood.

. . . . .

> *Caller:* I have a son that's a policeman in Bent Luke's metropolitan Missouri.
>
> *Operator:* What did you need, ma'am?
>
> *Caller:* I need to let him know I'm on my way home from Colorado.

. . . . .

> *Caller:* I parked my car in a spot that says "Truck Loading and Unloading Only, Tow-away Zone." What is going to happen to my car?

. . . . .

> *Caller:* A neighbor's tree fell on my house. The neighbors are not home. Will I get sued if I cut it up?

. . . . .

> *Caller:* Will the police drive me to work?

. . . . .

> *Caller:* I left my car in a ditch, and I'm now at home. Can

I get an officer to stop by my car and grab the presents I left in it and bring them to me?

. . . . .

Caller: Can you look in the reverse phone book and give me the phone numbers for all of my mom's neighbors?

. . . . .

Caller: Puget Power's recording needs to be updated. Can you call and let them know?

. . . . .

Caller: Can you unplug my coffeepot I left on at my house?

. . . . .

Caller: Could you send someone over here and have them help me put my tire chains on? I bought some today, but I don't know how to put them on!!

. . . . .

Caller: Hi, it's Veronica. Anything going on?

. . . . .

Caller: When is my son's flight arriving?

. . . . .

Caller: My cable's out. It's been out. Any idea when it's going to be back on?

. . . . .

Caller: I saw paw prints in the snow leading to my deck. What should I do about it?

. . . . .

Caller: Please connect me to Switzerland.

. . . . .

Caller: I've got a roach stuck in my ear.

. . . . .

Caller: I'd like to make a unanimous complaint, so don't use my name.

. . . . .

Caller: Am I talking to a real person, or is this a recording?

. . . . .

Caller: Is it OK for a civilian to take a person to the hospital, or does the ambulance have to do it?

. . . . .

Caller: (irate, when asked to spell his name) That's "W" as in "Williams" and "Y" as in "why."

. . . . .

Caller: He's not breathing!
Operator: Can you get the phone close to him?
Caller: Why? You want to hear he's not breathing, too?

. . . . .

Operator: Does she have any weapons?
Caller: Well, she has real long fingernails.

. . . . .

Operator: We'll need a description of him.
Caller: He's a lawyer.

. . . . .

Caller: Do you work the night shift?
Operator: I am tonight. Do you have an emergency I can help you with?
Caller: No. But would you give me a wake-up call at

6:00 A.M.? I have an important doctor's appointment tomorrow.

. . . . .

Caller: Hi, my new wife left me and took all my clothes.
Operator: OK, we can send an officer to take a theft report.
Caller: Could you have the officer stop and get a pizza on his way over?

Stupid Moments in Defecation

Give a hand for American ingenuity, which, in the cases that follow, takes a relatively basic act (i.e., defecation) and applies it (often literally) in new and unique venues.

Here we commemorate those moments involving defecation as a form of protest, as a means of retribution, or simply as an unusually stupid act.

Defecation on Books as Protest

An Ohio man used defecation as a novel form of protest (protest against *what* is a bit unclear) when he "did his duty" on at least 40 different public-library books that had as their subjects homosexuality, the United Nations, or the Federal Reserve. The books were found in the men's toilet or book-return area in different Dayton, Ohio, area libraries.

The man, who works at an Air Force base and also owns a bookstore specializing in Catholic books, was arrested. He pleaded no contest to two counts of criminal damaging, and owed $518 in restitution. He will also probably lose his library card. As Municipal Judge Bill Littlejohn said, "I certainly think he should not go to the library."

Defecation in Art, Health Risks of

The New Museum of New York City was faced with a unique problem: How to ensure that a piece of defecating art would not endanger the art-loving public.

The work, *Cloaca* by Belgian artist Wim Delvoye, is a machine that duplicates the entire human digestion process. Viewers feed the machine spaghetti (for example) in one end, and feces eventually come out the other. (According to the artist, "One really can watch the bacteria doing their work in the bowels.")

The museum needed permission from the U.S. Department of Health and Human Services before they could show the piece in January 2002. The Health Department gave its OK, but only after it was assured that the museum would seal the "dung hole" in a glass container and that each piece that came out of the machine would be removed "instantly" by a guard wearing plastic gloves. The artist commented, "They have become so afraid from everything to do with bacteria they've ordered strict regulations. . . . Everything will be sealed off from nasty smells. The Health Departments asked us also to give a certificate that the dung is really human and doesn't contain diseases."

Defecation by Athletes, Mischievous

Green Bay Packer Najeh Davenport used to be a University of Miami football star. But it was his actions off the gridiron and in the closet that got him in the news in 2002. Johnson was arrested after a female student at Barry University said she woke up in the middle of the night in her dorm room and found Johnson in her closet—defecating in her laundry basket. He was arrested and charged with one count of criminal mischief and one count of burglary. His attorney, Richard Sharpstein, noted that the charges were to be dismissed in exchange for Davenport teaching a series of football clinics. In an interesting choice of language, he added, "Thanks to the plea deal, it won't be necessary for us to dig to the bottom of this situation, and we're going to leave it where it was."

Defecation by Principals for No Apparent Reason

A former police dispatcher in Pocatello, Idaho, wanted to get to the bottom of his problem: On Sundays over several months, he kept finding human feces in his front yard. He set up a camera and finally got photos of the perpetrator: a 46-year-old female elementary-school principal. She was charged with misdemeanor trespass and admitted in a pretrial conference that she had defecated 21 times on that particular lawn . . . as well as 5 times on neighbors' lawns. There was no explanation for her activity.

Defecation by Others as a Means of Making Money

A Memphis robber discovered the almost perfect victim: a man sitting on a public toilet, defecating.

The man we'll call John Doe was in a toilet in an East Memphis office building when the robber stuck his head under the door and demanded his wallet. As the victim testified: "He grabbed my ankles and started to pull me out of the stall into the main area of the men's room. I was making a lot of noise. I was yelling for help. I was both scared and angry. My left pant leg came off, and I think he realized by its weight that what came with that was my wallet."

The robber ran off and was caught by security guards in the parking lot. He was later convicted of robbery, perhaps due, in part, to the prosecutor's statement to the jury: "One of the times we are most vulnerable as victims of crimes is in a toilet stall with pants down. That is when the defendant chose to make John Doe a victim."

Defecation Used to Comment on One's Arrest

A Medford, Oregon, car dealer watching a football game at Spiegelberg Stadium was said to be drunk and causing a disturbance. Medford police took him to the county's detox unit, and the man allegedly resisted arrest by yelling, poking, and hitting the officers there. Then, in the jail's clothing-exchange room, where inmates strip off their street clothes and are given jail clothing, he defecated on the floor.

He was later taken to the shower, where he allegedly defecated again and threw what resulted at the two deputies there—hitting one on his uniform and the other on his face, arms, and hands. (The man claims this wasn't the case. He says that he was beaten to a pulp, which affected his bowel control, and that he refused to shower because he wanted people to see how he was treated.) He was released on bail—which also included an extra $40 to cover a mattress that was smeared with his feces.

Unsolved Defecation Mysteries

This is a little-known and little-explored area of American justice. Two of the more compelling cases:

The Strange Case of the Water Tower Defecator

Bucolic White Bear Township in Minnesota has been plagued by a nocturnal defecator. For months, police have found human feces and soiled toilet paper (or substitutes therefor) near a water tower—but no perpetrator of said leavings. The police have set up a motion detector and two floodlights, assigned a deputy near the tower, and added a patrol. But to no avail. The crime remains unexplained, and the perp is still at large.

The Mysterious Case of the College Campus Crapper

Beginning in May 1999, San Francisco University was attacked by a serial defecator. An unknown person or persons caused twenty-four separate defecation incidents—leaving feces on the floors of bathrooms (both men's and women's) around the campus and even once on a classroom floor. Despite heightened efforts by campus security, the culprit eluded capture. Wally Simmons, manager of campus security operations, commented that the defecator was clever enough to change locations often and even showed no specific consistency in where he or she defecated, "but more often than not it's in the stall right in front of the toilet."

"It's pretty disgusting," he summed up.

And . . . one more unsolved dung mystery:

The Case of the Unidentified Flying Dung

Spattered dung was found on two sides of a house, in the backyard, and in a hot tub in Richfield, Utah, according to *The Salt Lake Tribune* in March 2001. "There were spatter marks every three or four inches. It was quite a mess," said an investigating scientist with the state Department of Health. And here's the mystery: The spattered dung was devoid of the tell-tale blue chemicals that indicate origin in an airplane. So health officials are baffled: Where did the dung rain down from?

Stupid American Toilet Problems

We're probably one of the cleanest peoples on earth and the most hygienic. One big reason: We take our toilet facilities seriously. Visitors say they marvel at our clean toilets and at our penchant for bathing and cleanliness. In fact, America can confidently boast it has the best toilet facilities of any large nation on earth. But there are times when things don't go so smoothly in the great American bathroom. . . .

Sometimes our toilets give way

Coolidge Winsett, age 75, was trapped for almost three days at the bottom of his outhouse in Virginia, crying out: "God, don't let me die like this!"

He had built the outhouse—made of oak planks over a dirt pit—back in 1950. One day in August 2000, after he went inside the floor finally gave way and he was trapped, suspended over the "bad stuff" by a subfloor. There, for three days he endured all sorts of crawling insects, maggots, and spiders in the darkness—and once, a rat. "I compare it to the Bible's hell," he said vividly. Finally, a postal worker noticed accumulating mail in Winsett's mailbox and went out back, where he heard a faint voice. Together with emergency crews, the postal worker rescued the man in the pit.

"It wasn't pretty," he said. A local woman summed it up in a poem she wrote praising the action of the postal worker: "God sent an angel, just in time, when Mr. Winsett, someone needed to find."

Not all of us use our wonderful American toilet facilities

A man from Fond du Lac, Wisconsin, was recently awakened by a man about to go on his living-room floor. He had been awakened in the middle of the night by a banging and clanging: There was an intruder in his house! Arming himself with a baseball bat, he went into the living room, where he found the intruder . . . getting ready to urinate on the floor. The man did the only thing he could do: He told him to use the toilet.

Afterward, the man was arrested. He claimed he had the wrong house: He had thought he was about to urinate in his boss's living room.

Sometimes our toilets simply explode

At a large plumbing convention, held in Fort Worth in October 2002, an attendee and his wife went into their hotel bathroom when suddenly, without warning, the toilet exploded, shooting debris all over the room—contaminating the bathroom and the clothing of the convention-goer and his wife. Apparently, exploding toilets are nothing new—a fact not lost on fellow plumbing conventioneers.

"It was quite humorous because it happened to a consultant who was famous for conducting a study about exploding toilets," said Stanley Wolfson, event planner for the American Society of Plumbing Engineers. "I mean, really, what are you going to do if you can't laugh about an exploding toilet?"

Sometimes we have to pay as we go

Taking the kids for a day at the museum? If you're at the Wisconsin Historical Museum, bring a few extra bills. When the inevitable time comes when one of your charges tugs on your sleeve and says he or she has to go right NOW, be prepared to shell out $3.00 (a dollar more if *you* get the urge). That's the price the museum now charges patrons to use their public (and we're using the word loosely) toilets. "The impetus, unfortunately, is money, or a lack thereof," explained the museum's director.

Sometimes, we share our bathrooms— but don't want to

In March 1995, the city of San Diego was sued because of its unisex bathroom policy at the Jack Murphy Stadium. During a Billy Joel and Elton John concert, an audience member felt the call. He went first to one bathroom but, seeing that it was unisex, he decided to go to another. The next bathroom was also unisex. Feeling that he just couldn't go in a bathroom with women in it, he asserted he "had to hold it in for four hours." And so he sued for pain and suffering.

Sometimes, our toilets are very, very expensive

In 1993, the National Aeronautic and Space Agency spent $23 million for a prototype toilet for our astronauts in outer space. The cost got so high in part because astronauts rejected the first model—they wanted a manual flush instead of automatic flushing. And $7 million was tacked on by the maker, United Technologies Hamilton Standard, to make the toilet fully manually operational. During flights of the space-shuttle *Endeavor,* Mission Control had to remind the astronauts something they'd probably heard on earth before: Keep the toilet lid down when not in use.

And sometimes, the government gets involved where it shouldn't

In 1992, the federal Occupational Safety and Health Administration raided the offices of the Pro-Line Cap company and demanded it do something about having too few toilets for its 30 female employees. So the cash-strapped company, anxious to comply with federal law, fired all thirty women.

Times When You Probably Should Keep Your Mouth Shut

We Americans are known as a friendly people, anxious to share our names, our ideas and passions, our essential friendliness, with our fellow citizens. There are times, however, when maybe it would be better to keep our mouths shut. . . .

- Illinois prison guard Michael Moreci, caught in a traffic jam, decided to vent his frustration at a fellow driver. He shouted angrily, "I beat up guys like you for a living!" The driver turned out to be a federal judge, Sam Amirante. His passenger was the wife of a Chicago Bears lineman. Fortunately, Moreci was merely arrested.

- A Manhattan salesman waved a $50 bill in front of the face of a woman riding the elevator in his apartment building, thinking she was the prostitute he had called to his apartment on the telephone. She wasn't. She was a prosecutor in the Brooklyn D.A.'s office. She had him arrested for sexual assault.

- An Ohio man decided to call a phone-sex chat line. He dialed and then started talking, using what may politely be termed sexually explicit language. He kept it up for 15 to 20 minutes, long enough for the person on the receiving end to have the call traced via another line. That person, it turned out, was not a phone-sex worker at all, and the number was not that of a phone-sex line. Instead, it belonged to Chief Guy Turner—of the Cleveland police. Turner was not amused to have some unknown man calling in obscenities on his home phone. Turner sent some of his officers to the man's home, where he had finally shut up: He had fallen asleep still holding the phone. He was awakened and arrested.

Stupid Sex in America

Woody Allen once said, "Sex is the most fun you can have without laughing." We beg to differ. Sometimes laughter is an integral part, as of course is stupidity. . . .

Sex at Teter

October 2002. Teter residence hall, Indiana University. A man dressed in a fuzzy bear or a beaver costume. Young women rushing up and exposing themselves to him. A hall manager further reports seeing cameras and nude women walking the hallways. This was all not the norm at good old Teter Hall. The story finally came out: According to the campus newspaper, a California porno-film company was shooting on campus. The president of Teter residence hall commented to the Indiana *Daily Student*: "I just think it's a shame. We try to promote this fun atmosphere in a positive sense and something like this happens and it can ruin your reputation." Poor Teter.

Family Park Oral-Sex Show

On the night of July 17, 2000, a young 20-something couple visiting Paramount's King's Island Park in Cincinnati, Ohio, saw a photo booth. The young man, according to the police report, "casually mentioned to his girlfriend that she could give him oral sex" there. They went inside the photo booth and started at it, not realizing that outside the booth was a monitor, so that all passersby, including little children, could watch the action. After several minutes, the couple realized what was happening. The man ran outside and tried to cover the image of the monitor with his hands, but it was too late. The couple was arrested.

Said a spokesperson for the park: "We're a family park and try to operate and maintain a family experience." This was not a family experience.

Fireman Featured in Hot Porn

Good natured fireman John McMahan was angry—and probably will never brush his teeth before a camera again. In 2003, he announced he was suing the producers. It began when he and some fellow firefighters noticed a group of young people who looked like students, carrying a video camera. McMahan greeted the students, who said they needed help in a treasure hunt. They then handed McMahan a brush and toothpaste and asked him to brush his teeth. McMahan good-naturedly complied, while the students filmed. He found out later that he was now a featured actor in *Shane's World29: Frat Row Scavenger Hunt3*—a hot new porno movie. McMahan's lawyer said he was "humiliated and embarrassed."

Army Porn

It was probably not what the U.S. military had in mind, although there *was* a military theme. Viewers in Webster, New York, near Rochester, were watching *Army Newswatch*, a program produced by the U.S. Army, when suddenly on came a gay-porn show. It lasted about 20 minutes. Cable-television operators were baffled as to how it got on the air. On the positive side, some viewers who called in noted that the show did have a military theme—it involved an older officer and some younger men. It was the wrong army though: the German.

Incompetent Peeping

A unusually incompetent George Washington High School student, in Charleston, West Virginia, was allegedly tempted by the girl's locker room and decided to get a peep or two. He snuck inside and stationed himself between a short brick wall near the showers and the piping behind it. When the coast was clear, he then hoisted himself up on an ice machine to reach the top of the wall, which was about a foot and a half lower than the ceiling. Here his problems began; he thought he made eye contact with a female student, and he became startled; he then slipped; and he became trapped behind the shower wall. The student here showed some coolness under pressure. He did not shout or call attention to himself. He simply waited until school let out and then used his cell phone to call his father, who proceeded to come to the school, where he partially tore down the wall and got his son out. At home, the father called the school and told them what had happened.

Harry Potter and the Magic Vibrator

September 2002 reports in the *New York Post* and the Toronto *Star*, quoting parents' website "reviews" of the Mattel Nimbus 2000 plastic-replica broomstick from the latest Harry Potter movie, highlighted its battery-powered special effect: vibration. Wrote a Texas mother: "I was surprised at how long [my daughter and her friends] can just sit in her room and play with this magic broomstick." Another said her daughter fights her son for it but complains that "the batteries drain too fast." A New Jersey mother, sensing a problem, said her daughter could keep playing with it, "but with the batteries removed." Still another mother, age 32, said she enjoyed it as much as her daughter.

Ultimate Revenge

A flasher in Virginia Beach, Virginia, was doing what flashers normally do, exposing himself—in this case to a 12-year-old schoolgirl. But this flasher picked the wrong schoolgirl and the wrong elevator in which to do his flashing. As he exposed himself, the girl kept her cool—and reached over and grabbed the zipper on his pants . . . and zipped it up. Police say the man probably suffered serious injuries, and they searched area hospitals for people checking in with severe penile damage.

⭐

BREAST ENLARGEMENT—NOT FOR HUMANS ONLY

No one wants a "peanut udder" teat—so what's a cow or her breeder to do? Cow breeders want to win, particularly at the big fairs where cows are exhibited. "When I explain to city friends, I say these are like Miss America pageants," explains one dairy farmer. And so modern science has stepped in: injections of isobutane gas to enhance the cow udders and liquid silver protein to make them smooth, plump, and less wrinkled. "What they're trying to do is make both rear quarters absolutely equal, both 36 double D. People really hate it when I compare cows to humans, but it's kind of the same."

But that's viewed as cheating by some. All-natural udders are preferred, and so judges and vets are fighting back. According to the *Milwaukee Journal Sentinel*, University of Wisconsin vets have now developed a way to use ultrasound to reveal udder implants and enhancements.

And there's an added benefit. According to vet Robert O'Brien, "We think we could clean up the Miss America contest with the same technology."

What Average Americans Really Think: Fascinating Facts from Polls

- Percentage of New Jersey residents who believe in ESP: 63%

  Percentage who believe in the theory of evolution: 53%

  Percentage of New Jersey residents who believe there is life on other planets: 56%

  Percentage who believe medical doctors are "usually right": 45%

—2000 statewide survey by Rutgers University and the Newark *Star-Ledger,* as printed in *The Washington Post,* April 17, 2000

• Number of Americans who believe they have been abducted by aliens: 20 million

—*The Washington Post,* April 17, 2000

• According to Zogby International, a PR firm, Republicans prefer Coke over Pepsi, 45 to 33 percent. Democrats prefer Pepsi, 41 to 37 percent.

Dead Americans

"Old soldiers never die, they just fade away," said our great American general Douglas MacArthur to the U.S. Congress, shortly before trying to do the opposite and run for president.

These were stirring yet poignant words, and we should perhaps reflect on them, but they have nothing to do with what follows, which are stupid ways not of how Americans die but of what happens after they die.

Personalized hobby caskets for dead hobbyists

Being dead is dull enough, so one funeral casket company, Southern Caskets Direct, recently had the great idea of personalizing its casket stock with bright lithographed designs and catchy titles of favorite hobbies. Are you (or more appropriately, were you) a racing fan? How about a "The Race Is Over" casket with a checkered flag and whizzing cars emblazoned on it? Were you a golfer? How about the "Fairway to Heaven" casket, painted to look like a gold putting green?

HOW TO BE A RICH CORPSE

Let the poor and the middle-class opt for the plebeian ceme-
tery plots or urns. Now the wealthy have a better option: the
12-story, earthquake-proof, $190 million Roman Catholic
Cathedral of Our Lady of the Angels.

This Los Angeles church boasts special private crypts—
ranging in price from $50,000 to $3 million.

Mourners can park for a mere $12 a day and also buy a
bottle of the pleasant house Chardonnay in the church gift
shop—for only $24.99.

Are you a former postal worker, or do you just plain love a
good joke? How about a casket that looks like a brown-
paper package, has the deceased's last address on it, and is
stamped . . . RETURN TO SENDER.

Amateur Funeral Homes

People complain about the high prices funeral homes
charge for burial—however, there's an alternative: the amateur funeral home. The Wade Funeral Home of New
Haven, Connecticut, is one such company; it was accused in
2001 of operating without a license and disposing of bodies
in a somewhat unusual but certainly low-cost manner:
They stored them in the garage. In fact, it was presumably
the smell of the decomposing bodies in the garage that led
police there—they found five of them, some of which had
been there at least three years.

No Pay? No Bury!

If you want to be buried by the Hathaway-Peterman Funeral Home of Hickory County, Missouri, you had better

DEATH PRODUCTS WE CAN LIVE WITHOUT . . .

Death Row Marv: an amusing action figure with eyes that light up when he sits in the electric chair ($28.95). The writing on the box says, "Watch Marv convulse as the switch is thrown, then hear him say, 'That the best you can do?'"

make sure you or your loved ones have sufficient money to pay the bill. Nancy King apparently didn't have sufficient funds to pay Hathaway-Peterman for her boyfriend's cremation, so the home did the natural (but alas, illegal) thing: They dumped the body back on her porch. "I had to go out to get a gallon of milk. When we came home I started to turn in the driveway [and] I saw this white bag on my porch. I knew exactly what it was," said King. State regulators pointed out that there were "a number of recourses the funeral director could have taken other than taking the body back and putting it on the porch."

The Old-School-Colors Casket

Some people never let you forget they went to Harvard or good old Penn State. For them, Collegiate Memorials, a Macon, Georgia, company, is heaven-sent. It sells caskets that can be adorned with the old school colors and logos of 40 colleges. The most popular caskets? Nebraska Cornhusker and Tennessee. According to the company president, "Right now, this is probably a breath of fresh air for the funeral industry."

About The Authors

KATHRYN PETRAS and ROSS PETRAS are siblings, and the authors of the national bestselling "Stupidest" series as well as other humor books. Their titles include *The 776 Stupidest Things Ever Said, Stupid Sex, Stupid Celebrities,* and *Very Bad Poetry.* Their work has received the attention of such personalities as David Brinkley and Howard Stern, publications including *The New York Times, Playboy, Cosmopolitan, The Washington Post,* and the London *Times,* and TV series including *Good Morning America.* They are also the creators of the number one bestselling *365 Stupidest Things Ever Said Page-A-Day Calendar* (now in its tenth year).